FALLING INTO FLOWERS

By Lynne Barnes

BLUE LIGHT PRESS ❖ 1ST WORLD PUBLISHING

1ST WORLD
PUBLISHING

SAN FRANCISCO ❖ FAIRFIELD ❖ DELHI

FALLING INTO FLOWERS
Copyright ©2017 by Lynne Barnes

1ST WORLD LIBRARY
PO Box 2211
Fairfield, IA 52556
www.1stworldpublishing.com

BLUE LIGHT PRESS
www.bluelightpress.com
Email: bluelightpress@aol.com

BOOK & COVER DESIGN
Melanie Gendron
www.melaniegendron.com

COVER ART
"California Poppies" by Carole D. Hay

AUTHOR PHOTOGRAPH
Carole D. Hay

FIRST EDITION

Library of Congress Control Number: 2016963443

ISBN 9781421837703

Praise for Lynne Barnes' Writing

"Lynne Barnes' writing is intensely empathetic; she's a wounded healer to an orbit of beautiful broken souls. She is a hearth keeper to her life stories, stories that intersect with San Francisco, commune living, same-sex love, and social justice. There is a steady rhythm of longing from a choir of voices in this book, and every poem burns with unwavering hope."

—Scott Caputo, Author of *Holy Trinity of Chiles*

"It takes a certain kind of daring to write a memoir in poetry – the author must possess confidence, a powerful memory and a grace with words that will capture the reader's imagination. Luckily, Lynne Barnes has all these qualities. Her lyrical language draws you into many different worlds — from the cotton fields and blackberry brambles of a Southern childhood, to a gritty New York psychiatric ward, to a hippie commune in the Haight-Ashbury, with many surprising stops along the way. Barnes carves images as sharp and luminescent as gemstones. Her well-examined life makes for a compelling and vibrant story."

—Elaine Elinson, Author of *Wherever There's a Fight: How Runaway Slaves, Strikers, Suffragists, Immigrants, and Poets Shaped Civil Liberties in California* (with Stan Yogi) Gold Medal Award Winner, California Book Awards, 2010

"*Falling into Flowers* invokes a powerful sense of history, sculpted with tender, goose-bump evoking details, depicting the South in the 1950s and '60s and the Haight-Ashbury commune scene after the Summer of Love. This book is a journey from marshes of grief into flats full of idealistic hippies in the City of St. Francis in the '70s and '80s… and twenty-five years beyond. Along the way, the author meets a few of the people and witnesses some of the events that helped shape this era of The Flower Generation. Lynne Barnes writes poems that sing like ballads. Her language is gorgeous and devastating."

—Diane Frank, Author of *Blackberries in the Dream House*

"I met Lynne Barnes through my *Poets 11* anthology series as Poet-in-Residence for the San Francisco Public Library. She has emerged through our city's bohemian/hippie movements to write some of the most profoundly progressive poetry of this generation."

—Jack Hirschman, Poet Laureate of San Francisco, 2006-2008

"Startling images and luminescent language lead us on a journey from the South to the 'countercultural tornado' of the late 1960s and '70s. Despite despair and darkness, hope for a more compassionate world keeps the reader moving through different landscapes. Ultimately, this collection is about grace, counting your blessings, and the power of love and nature to heal 'the invisible scars.'"

—Louise Nayer, Author of *Burned* (*Oprah Magazine* "Great Read," 2010), re-issued 2016

"Thankfully, Lynne Barnes gifted me her poem 'Postcard from the Castro' after one of my lectures about my friend Harvey Milk, and I instantly fell in love with her succinct and enchanted poem about him. The exchange was in the great bohemian tradition of soul sharing that is our mutual legacy of growing up in San Francisco's counter-culture. I love too, finding that *Falling Into Flowers* is so adeptly steeped in the history of literature and poetry. I am quite certain I will be randomly opening this book to any page for daily inspiration for many years to come!"

—Dan Nicoletta, *LGBT: San Francisco* (2017), Dan's first collection of iconic photography documenting forty years of the LGBT civil rights movement, starting when he stepped into Harvey Milk's Castro Camera shop in the mid-1970s, at age nineteen.

"Lynne Barnes' poetic memoir, *Falling into Flowers*, is a bouquet of raw honesty. This astonishing collection invites the reader to open all senses and experience each poem-petal. With courage and beauty, she takes us through her garden of Southern roots, from 'Cotton Fields and Cuckoo's Nests' to a 'Winter of Love.' *Fall into* (her) *river of images* where *the scent of flower-filled trees in February will bulldoze* (you) *back to a time* of vulnerability, adventure, and strength."

—Loretta Diane Walker, Author of *Word Ghetto* and *In This House,* Winner of the 2016 Phyllis Wheatley Award for Poetry

*Publishing a volume of poetry
is like dropping a rose petal down the Grand Canyon
and waiting for the echo.*

—Don Marquis, 1878-1937
author of *archy* and *mehitabel*

Acknowledgements

Grateful acknowledgement is made to the following publications where these poems or previous versions of them first appeared.

Feather Floating on the Water: Poems for Our Children: "*Tulipa humilis*"

The Gathering 13: Ina Coolbrith Circle Poetry Anthology 2015-2016: "Sunday in the Temple of Democracy"

Mediphors: "Charlotte's Web"

Poets 11: An Anthology of Poems from the San Francisco Poets 11 Reading Series, 2007: "Morning," "Winter of Love"

Poets 11: An Anthology of Poems from the San Francisco Poets Eleven Reading Series 2008: "In That Sleep of Death," "The Poet at Five," "Simple Pleasures"

Poets 11: 2012: "Drawing Joseph Out About Stonewell," "Soul's Flora," "St. Frances of Augusta"

Poets 11 Anthology: 2014: "Bijou of New Orleans," "The Call of the West," "Sunday in the Temple of Democracy"

Poets 11 Anthology: 2016: "The Leaves of the Linden Tree," "Postcard from the Castro," "Stone Mountain"

Rain City Review: "Vigil"

River of Earth and Sky: Poems for the Twenty-First Century: "Grief"

Contents

IV. Children of the Dream

V. Mid-Life Kiss

VI. Witness

VII. Winter of Love

I

Cotton Fields and Cuckoo's Nests

This whole land, the whole South, is cursed, and all of us who derive from it,
whom it ever suckled, white and black both, lie under the curse.

—William Faulkner, "The Bear"

O magnet-South! O glistening perfumed South! my South!
O quick mettle, rich blood, impulse and love! Good and evil!
O all dear to me!

—Walt Whitman, from *Leaves of Grass*

...see the shaky future grow familiar
in the pinched, indigenous faces
of these thoroughbred mental cases...

—Robert Lowell, "Waking in the Blue"

The Poet at Five

after Larry Levis ("The Poet at Seventeen," from *Winter Stars*)

My childhood? I see it from beneath
the sunk down brim of my granddaddy's
sweat-scented, World War I-era wool cap,
borrowed for a morning that opens in neon black:

electric first-morning-ever rising before the sun,
a morning I can still touch after over sixty years,
morning when his hat protects me from splinters
of light as they begin to break from the sky's edge.

The strap my grandmother has sewn onto a flour sack
hangs across my shoulder and chest
like a military sash. My sack is a miniature
of the long, trailing bags the adults wear.

Blackberry grenades explode on my tongue, and wet
green leaves slap my cheeks as we walk single file
down a footpath through the woods, with honeysuckle
aromas dissolving in cool Spanish moss mist.

At the end of our journey, a white field shimmers
through the trees, and the sky is Mercurochrome.
My imagination is lit— I hear bluebells tinkle
as they brush against my legs.

From the cool oak and pine spires, into the oven of cotton field:
July flies screech as I pry tufts from dry, brown fists that draw blood.
I sit down in the dirt at the end of the first row,
taste salt trickling down my face, feel

the weightlessness of the treasure in my sack, watch
the deep pains my mother and my grandparents take
with the plants on the land I do not know they do not own
as they bend, burn, pick, bleed, sweat, thirst: Georgia 1951.

Intimations of Mortality

Anybody who has survived his childhood has enough information about life to last him the rest of his days.
—Flannery O'Connor

Pecan trees canopy the sandy backyard
on the edge of a small town not too far
from Flannery's Andalusia.
The weathered porch that wraps around
the back of the house shelters a well,
and cows graze in the field behind it—
my grandparents' final sharecropping stop
before the nursing home.

I build floor-plan-only houses here in the sand,
sit in their gritty, furniture-less living rooms
with my cousin Walter. We chase Rex and Judy,
the hunting hounds, smash the first of the pecans
with granddaddy's hammer, defying the rule
from Mrs. Jordan's (pronounced Miz Jerden's) son
that we are not to touch the crop.
We are willing to risk the wrath of the grownups,
but in this cusp of summer to autumn,
a good pecan is hard to find.

As Walter naps; as granddaddy drives his mule,
steers his plow creating a furrow in the field
just beyond the cows, readying the earth
for cotton, corn, peas, tomatoes, and velvet beans;
as my grandmother adds a hickory stick to the wood stove,
preparing to bake her biscuits
in the kitchen where she spends her life,
I am alone on the spacious, gray back porch,
chasing a butterfly by Miz Jerden's bedroom window.

Her lacy curtain is open and I look up and see
a ninety-year-old naked by her bed,
as I stand embarrassed, transfixed,
my head just above her window sill.
I do not know that I will never forget
her cotton white body
covered in blue spider webs.

Sestina for the South

Hate is a wasteful emotion.
—Medgar Evers, Sergeant, United States Army
(Germany & France) 1943-1946

After thirty years, delayed justice
convicts de la Beckwith of the murder
of Medgar Evers, Mississippi black
man, martyr, whose spilled blood
washes over lush cottonwood green,
leaving a widow with a three-year-old child.

At thirty-one, Medgar's youngest boy,
born in a culture of injustice,
watches in an autopsy room as a copper green,
corroded coffin, exhumed, opens to a murdered
man, reveals, intact, the bloodless
body of his father, at peace, his black

face mirroring this grown child's age and blackness.
Son is father, father is son.
The child played on a driveway stained with blood,
where the father's ghost never knew justice.
For the child the father has been so long dead,
that in this tear-humid room, the inexperienced

son experiences his father's physical, young
self as if for the first time. His perfect black
body, lifeless, yet defying death,
offers solace for a wounded child—
a son learning of slow justice
bought with precious blood.

At five I ride a Southeastern Stages bus past silent, red
clay hills, my father driving, see blurred pine
scenery outside Monroe, Georgia, where injustice—
1946, the year I was born— lynched a black
veteran at Moore's Ford Bridge. Naive child,
I know nothing yet of race and death.

Crawfordville, Greensboro, Mon*roe,* my father's dead-
pan voice names our stops, never speaking of the blood,
as I worship him through the window of my childhood.
I roll along on a two-lane highway through emerald
hills toward Atlanta, past Taras, shanties. Black
faces in the back of the bus laugh (adjusted
to the injustice, the fear-ruled lives,
smothering dark tales of spilled blood),
as the green world rushes past a white child.

Cold Spell

My mother has just pulled her Red Velvet cake from the oven.
Its honeyed aroma reaches every corner of our home.
We huddle in the kitchen, the warmest place,
on this brittle November Saturday, 1950s Georgia.

I put away dishes as Henrietta sits on a tall stool
finishing her ham and collard greens. Today,
the top of the washing machine is her table,
where she sets down her plate
and slowly sips her sweet iced tea.

I love her sturdy presence when she first arrives,
the melodies she hums as she dusts and irons and scrubs.
I love the gleam of her teeth when she smiles at me,
the tingle I feel from the *hons* and *shugahs*
she sprinkles around me and my brother.
I want her to live with us all the time.

On this no-school late morning,
after fumbling with the knob on the outside door,
my brother backs into the kitchen,
wearing black, wool gloves and his heavy winter coat.
He's carrying a gray enamel pan in both hands,
pan that holds our twenty-five cent,
Woolworth's baby alligator, Al,
stiff as the ice panes clinking around him.

As we sit at the kitchen table, trying to befriend our grief,
we eat a piece of my mother's warm, crimson art
with its sugary glaze of white icing.
Then Henrietta's chocolate arms
lift our plates to the sink where she washes them,
whisper-singing one of her gospel hymns
while she stares out the steamy kitchen window
at something miles beyond
the pine and mimosa trees in our back yard.

Time Out

Remembering Dave Brubeck as he passes at age 91 (December 5, 2012)

I was always secretly falling for the women in trouble,
like Kathryn, who had lupus, who transferred to us
during our sophomore year, after a long hospital stay.
I loved her rush into the throb of the world around her,
smoking, drinking, having sex with the Second Lieutenants,
trying to experience everything before her likely-shortened
life ended.

She was the first student with headphones,
and she loved every kind of music and listened to it all
for nearly twenty-five years more before she died.
As I write, I am with her, sitting on the floor of her dorm room
passing those bulky headphones back and forth, alternating for hours
between *Time Out* and *Surrealistic Pillow,*
between "Take Five" and "Somebody to Love."

First Boyfriend

At Lake Olmstead, in his car, on a moonless night,
we kiss for the first time, lips just touching when
a policeman's flashlight frightens us apart.
We laugh later about this fragile moment
shattered by a beam of light. We bicycle
over gold leaves, stroll through spring azaleas
holding hands. We write English papers together
on rainy afternoons, and once, at a car hop drive-in,
I even try to tell him who I really am.

Every Friday evening in my mother's kitchen
we bake homemade pizza pie. Afterwards,
in the darkened living room, by the flicker of the TV,
I curl my legs onto the sofa, lay my head
against his chest, abandon my deeper self
for the comfort of just belonging somewhere.
His hand always trembles on my shoulder as he
draws me even closer, and on one of those nights
he asks me to marry him.

I fly to a job in New York instead,
and he eventually marries someone I don't know.
A few years later my mother phones to tell me
he's put a shotgun barrel into his mouth,
in front of his wife,
and with that tender, trembling hand
blasted an opening through the wall of his life.

First Girlfriend

Before you know kindness as the deepest thing inside,
you must know sorrow as the other deepest thing.
—Naomi Shihab Nye

With each new song, you unwrap
the silver capo's elastic strap, tighten it
around the guitar's neck, change key,
hands moving with swan grace,
strumming beneath your smoked-glass voice,
eyes soft candles in the campfire light,
or dark, haunted house windows,
as you fidget the capo in both hands,
trying to name fragments of your trauma
out loud, failing… finally handing me
your stories in a letter one day.

My image shines like a full moon
in the mirror of your face.
I come of age with you, leave
the ledge I have been living on.
I run from school to find you
on the day Kennedy is shot.

One kiss, then six years
of a Simon and Garfunkel-scored
platonic friendship,
before touching each other again,
one July Georgia night,
as moonlight silks through pine boughs,
burnishing the windowsill,
and cricket's wings sing in gardenia air.

We part the next morning,
me slipping off to be maid of honor

at a friend's wedding out of town,
you asking me not to go.
I am so over the moon,
I do not see danger here on Earth.

Two days later, when I am with you again,
I put your capo into your hand,
my fingers tracing the edge
of the powder burn,
as images swarm like insects,
eat my holiest memories
into ragged lace.

You scrubbed on neuro cases, knew
temple, not mouth, was sure.
You swallowed pills for courage,
in your empty, newly-rented
apartment on Winter Street,
on that sizzling summer afternoon,
just days before Neil Armstrong
walked on the moon.

You never really had a chance
with a murderous mother who tried to hang you,
a torturing foster who beat you with a rubber hose,
a bullying orphanage, all palimpsest beneath
your same sex attraction.

I held you then, I carry you still…
next kisses draw blood,
pressing against your shards
imbedded in my lips— your
fine crystal smithereened
into a thousand jagged bits
of dazzling, imploded rage.

Southern Schooling

I. Medical College

There is no agony like bearing an untold story inside you.
—Zora Neale Hurston, *Dust Tracks on a Road*

The mornings begin at half past five
in the hospital cafeteria.
Bacon, eggs, coffee, grits,
as starch-stiff stratosphere gray hems
kiss our calves.

We are on call for births,
turn quadriplegic teens,
after no-helmet catastrophes,
on frames that embrace them
like basketed meat ready for grills.

Rattling lungs call us to suction machines
where we plunge tubes into necks
of cancer patients with tracheotomies.

New diabetics listen
while we teach them to give themselves shots,
after we practice
on oranges, our thighs, each other's arms.

We visit the state asylum,
find a twelve-year-old
African American autistic girl, Earline,
mixed in on a back ward, with women
who had lobotomies in the forties.

The dean decrees we sit through
Miss Lily's Charm School
where the world shrinks to the size of a hand
stuffed into a white glove holding a teacup,
and she makes us mix at Second Lieutenant parties
with boys from Fort Gordon,
just before they ship out to Vietnam.

Inside this swirl, I am in love,
not with one of the soldiers,
but with one of the girls:

Secret electricity sparks inner, blissful, candlelit miracle.
Butterfly rises from chrysalis, but wings shrivel, trapped
in an ambient, mossback haze that hovers as a smog never lifting.
This psychic monoxide changes the locks in my bloodstream.
After a while, all circuits fail. It is hard to eat, hard to care.

II. Public Health

We each one of us somehow caught all by ourself...
I'm caught worse than you is...
Because I am Black... because I am colored.
    —Carson McCullers, *The Member of the Wedding*

With my aging public health professor, Miss Culpepper,
I cross the railroad tracks at Fifth and Gwinnett,
visit a mother and newborn just home from a hospital birth.
An ice-tinged February wind pushes us from behind,
past puddles and trash, to a weather-grayed shack—
the last along a pot-holed dirt lane.
In heavy coats, black bags in our blue-gloved hands,
we come to stairs with missing steps, front door with no knob,
window with rag crammed into an empty pane.
A small black boy in a thin beige jacket lets us in
where a frightened toddler holds the rusty bars of an iron bed.

The mother lies on a naked mattress gone yellow with age,
holds her newborn wrapped in the blue blanket they sent him home in.
She wears a layer of clothes, a faded pink housecoat over that, a blank
    face,
as small gusts of wind whistle their way inside,
and we form small white clouds with our mouths
that rush toward each other, then disappear.

We peel back the infant's blanket to check his shriveling cord,
and I watch Miss Culpepper after she asks about bedclothes.
After forty years at this, she no longer registers emotion,
while I have trouble with composure
as the mother points to paper blankets— newspapers—
open at the bottom of the bed and crumpling against the wall
in this unpainted, unheated, godforsaken, one-room home.

A raw wind blasts our faces as we open the no-knob front door,
step carefully down the broken stairs, and walk away.

Back in the dorm, as the sun goes down,
I grab a bottle of aspirin, open a Coke, and head outside.
Swirls of pastel paint smear the sky, pine needles
skirl in the wind, crow's screams rise.

Invisible poison fog that cannot speak its name,
blistering mustard gas of racism: war on all fronts.
I stumble through my own embattled ruins
to a field behind the nursing school,
lift my cold-numbed palm
for communion
with a mountain of tiny white moons.

Here in the icy, darkening grass,
not too far from the railroad tracks,
I swallow the night.

From Bluebird Road

She did not know why she was sad, but because of this peculiar sadness,
she began to realize she ought to leave the town.
—Carson McCullers, *The Member of the Wedding*

There was a time when the silky touch of cool, green
Charleston grass beneath my bare feet, when nectar pearls
from honeysuckle against my tongue, lazy winks
of lightning bugs, cries of whippoorwills, perfume of wisteria
were enough… yet even then, when I was four,

Maureen, the teenage daughter of the neighborhood grocer,
interrupted an escape attempt, rescued me,
pushed me home, just as I made it to the main road
on my tricycle. Where was it that I wanted to go?

As dogwood blossoms burst like popcorn, decorate
both sides of our street in white garlands, I play tag,
and slide in cardboard boxes down pine straw slicks
on the grounds of an old indigo plantation:
Fruitland Nurseries, acres of wild garden
one step over the boundary of my back yard.

Its pine woods, bamboo forest, camellia stand
cradle my shy schoolmate Janet's bedraggled,
Antebellum Era home, where we find
secret closets with ancient, musty dress-up clothes.

When frog-strangling rains drown the outside,
I fold into a crescent on the couch,
find Hidden Harbor with the Hardy Boys,
or climb into a roadster next to Nancy Drew,
listening to the silken murmur of downpour.

Fourteen houses in our little bluebird world,
a kid or two in almost every one. We are
street family, backyard sisters and brothers
huddling around a summer hearth—
a churn buried in ice and rock salt,
that gifts us peach ice cream
if we work hard enough.

We zig and zag in sugar rush,
on freshly mowed July backyards,
take turns as targets in games of dodge ball,
laughing, high on the fragrance of cut grass,
the chemistry of play, unstoppable, until
our silhouettes melt in the warm night air.

Winters we build quick newspaper fires,
at the school bus stop, to warm our hands,
while praying for snow, or at least iced roads,
to call us back to the slow-burning,
coal-fed fires, sighing inside our living rooms.

At age six, I like Ike and watch him glide
down two-lane Washington Road
into the Augusta National Golf Course
in his black Presidential limo.
At ten, Mary Beth Jennings and I listen to "Hound Dog"
and "Blue Suede Shoes" every Sunday afternoon
for hours after we do our homework. Summers
we sit through Elvis movies two or three times,
then sneak through the woods to the lock and dam,
spy on the boys skinny dipping.

After my mother starts work at the bank,
and my brother falls ill on a school morning,
my father drives Henrietta to us
from the neighborhood across town
where he sells life insurance.

On her first Saturday in our home,
I set a place for her at our dining room table,
and my mother takes me aside, tells me quietly,
Henrietta will eat lunch alone, in the kitchen,
off the top of the ironing board.

In this close world no one speaks
don't love same sex or different race,
don't question God or doubt
a man's place at the head of family,
but the air is humid with these notions,
and I am pine, no, magnolia,
trying to bloom in vain, bound, covered
in the lush green smother of kudzu.

I graduate from nursing school in 1968,
read a review of a Broadway play in *Time*,
take a job at a New York City psych ward,
where Marilyn felt imprisoned in 1961,
and Mary McCarthy conceived *The Group*,
where a famous poet's granddaughter
seeks sanctuary on my watch,
and all the staff clamor to be off
for three days of peace and music
in Woodstock, New York.
I date Woody Allen's jazz band mate, learn
about Sydney Bechet, sit in Janis' audience,*
pay no attention to Stonewall…

At twenty-two, as a late summer rainstorm pelts
my hometown airport, I climb a set of rollered stairs
into a prop jet bound for New York, trade
the blackberry briar prickle and snag of my first reality,
the copper fragrance of April rain sprinkling red clay;
chirr of cicadas sanding surfaces of August evenings;
azure morning glories twined around posts of sprawling

front porches; the taste of sweet, wild plums;
I trade these, and the silky touch of cool, green
Charleston grass beneath my bare feet,
for an eleven-dollar, must-be-okay-with-mud-spatter,
front row center orchestra ticket to
The American Tribal Love-Rock Musical, Hair.

*Sunday, February 23, 1969, Queens College Flushing

Payne Whitney Clinic

Religion and antics... I am now in the Payne Whitney Clinic... in the other half, the down half... unable to function, depressed.
—Robert Lowell, 1949, *The Letters of Robert Lowell*

They asked me to go quietly and I refused to move, staying on the bed so they picked me up by all fours, two hefty men and two hefty women, and carried me up to the seventh floor in the elevator.
—Marilyn Monroe, Letter to Dr. Greenson from Payne Whitney, 1961

1. Mr. Howard

You worked your way down from the seventh floor
with the patience of a chess master
after you were committed
following a failed attempt to hang yourself.
Your intractable depression
wore us all down over the months,
but you learned over time
all the right things to say to get to floor six,
one move closer to freedom, to checkmate.
When you asked for a three hour pass,
you feigned *fine* like a possum feigns *death*,
went out to the IRT and ended yourself
in front of a train on the A-Line,
fifteen minutes after you left.

2. Mr. Green

*If you give me a dime I'll give you ten thousand dollars
as soon as I get out I just need to make this one very important call
I think I have the answer that could save the men on the Pueblo,
please if you just let me make this one call to Johnson I won't tell
anyone that you let me do it where's my toothbrush did you
take it? I don't want any food but I'll take some coffee you think*

I care that it's three am? I'm gonna' fly with those boys around
the moon at Christmastime and I have to get out and get my
passport updated no I will not stop pacing they need me to help
win the war... please if you just give me a dime I'll give you
ten thousand tomorrow...

First clinical trials with lithium pluck you
from the top of the bipolar-coaster,
save you from death by manic exhaustion.

3. Mrs. Castro

Kill your children... gas them... the voices whispered,
as the mysterious black dahlia of schizophrenia
bloomed inside you. Your young children
go to live with their grandmother, who rescued them,
drove them to the emergency room, and we lock you
behind the elevator doors of the seventh floor,
by judge's order,
begin trying to silence the whisperers
the only way we know how:
stronger and stronger hammer hits of Thorazine,
as summer bleeds into autumn.

4. Dr. X

You were one of most caring of the therapists at the clinic,
and we had no idea you had your own
underground volcanic condition;
one morning I came to work and you were locked
in the seclusion room, hearing voices, babbling.

5. Three Days Off

I make sure I take all the Elavil on the first morning,
expecting that no one will look for me and that I will be
gone by the time anyone notices I am missing,

gone just one month after virgin tenderness turns to stone.
I fall into a river of images of your burned temple, burn
a scar onto my face touching the radiator next to the bed,
do not know, do not wake, but, on the morning of the third day,
I come to feeling ravenous, mood up,
go out into the bustle of New York City, have breakfast.

II

The Call of the West

Bohemia has never been located geographically,
but any clear day when the sun is going down, if you mount Telegraph Hill,
you shall see its pleasant valleys and cloud-capped hills
glittering in the West...
—Bret Harte

...The waters, mile on mile,
Foam-fringed with feathery white;
The beaconed fortress isle,
And Yerba Buena's light.
— "From Russian Hill," Ina Coolbrith,
First Poet Laureate of California, 1915

Where there is charity and wisdom, there is neither fear nor ignorance.
—Saint Francis of Assisi

On the Road

We are all wanderers on this earth.
Our hearts are full of wonder
and our souls are deep with dreams.
  —Gypsy Wisdom

The cab driver helps me lift my backpack
and my mod red and blue-daisied cloth suitcase
as he empties me on 42nd Street
at the largest bus stop in the nation,
the busiest bus station in the world.
After a year of nursing frail minds
on the Upper East Side of New York City,
I'm saying goodbye to the East River,
Greenwich Village, the Frick Museum,
carrying my square, date-stamped
pictures, April '69— cast of *Hair*
performing free in Central Park.

We lay over in Chicago
and I snap photos of the Chicago Seven
on the steps of the courthouse
the day before their trial begins.
I make out with a guy from the bus
when we break down for a few hours in Cheyenne.
Yellowstone is a blur of bursting water and chipmunks.

I stow my suitcase and hike down
to the bottom of the Grand Canyon,
sink like a failed soufflé
into the sand along the banks of the Colorado River,
worrying that every rustle is a heat-seeking rattlesnake
as I nestle into my sleeping bag in the starlit dark.
After a restless night, the sun steams me
out of the clamshell coma I closed into at five a.m.

I wake to discover I am whole, not torn
by hungry coyotes or wolves, or murdered
by coral snakes wrapped in the colors of the German flag.
What a wilderness wuss I am.

Instead, I am magnificently blessed
by the six-foot-five presence of Jim Whittaker,
the first American to climb to the top of Everest.
He drops from the cosmos, next to me at the river,
and after we talk, he leaps ahead of me on the trail
carrying my pack with him back up the canyon wall—
on this second half of his morning stroll,
before a naturalist's luncheon above us on the rim.
An easy-for-him, but deeply sweet kindness
remembered these forty-plus years down the road.

I later learn that this man who guided Bobby Kennedy
up a never-before-climbed, fourteen-thousand-foot high
peak in Canada named for his assassinated brother John,
this man who straddled Nepal and Tibet
to lift himself five miles up, into oxygen-less sky,
was (and still is, at age eighty-five) afraid of heights.

In my new home on the West Coast,
I return to a garden of fragile minds,
spreading a mulch of meds and compassion,
but only my own sense of helplessness grows.
At least the Langley Porter psych staff use first names,
and I thank the goddess I am not a *Miss* anymore.
No clueless formality as I try to build rapport
with the suicidal and paranoid.

By '71, I'm marching down Geary Boulevard
with one hundred and fifty-six thousand
Vietnam War-protesting souls.
I am only weeks from quitting my job,

signing up for a free university class
called *Finding a Way Out*,
heading with the gravitas of an astronaut,
the naiveté of a badge-earning Girl Scout,
toward an imagined, life-saving,
hippie-go-lucky life.

With Jim Whittaker's *nature's the best teacher*
humming in my head,
I vision quest down Highway 1 to Big Sur
and its Ventana Wilderness.
With nothing like the 185-mile, 29,000-foot-high
Everest trek in mind,
I climb two miles up a hot, dusty trail,
then roller coaster ten more
through the cool shade of bay,
Monterey pine, and redwood trees
to a hidden forest hot spring,
where I soak, then fall
into the cloud softness
of my army surplus sleeping bag,
trying to learn what's next in life
by leaving everything behind.

The Drinking Gourd

The Drinking Gourd on Laguna and Union
has been gone for over forty years—
it's now the storefront of an upscale jeweler,
this old folk club
where Balin found Kantner in '65,
where long-haired, knock-out lesbian
singer Cris Williamson
opened a year's worth of gigs in '69,
before her Olivia Records fame...
and kept me coming back,
sitting alone at a front table,
nursing a beer all night,
after nursing psych emergencies all day.
The film, *Inside Llewyn Davis*,
struck a match to the synapse that fired
this twinkle in time back to me.

Zookeepers

I saw the best minds of my generation… destroyed by madness, starving,
mystical, naked.
　　—Allen Ginsberg, 1955
　　　　(Journal notes written after a therapy session at Langley Porter
　　　　Neuropsychiatric Institute, San Francisco, California)

For months afterwards I would see him
dangling beneath the sun of a naked light bulb,
sheet wound around his neck like an angry cottonmouth—
this boy even the hardened staff had come to love,
guileless twenty-year-old bipolar who had just begun
to treat his depression with speed.

He was a million brain cells lighter
than when he came in at age seventeen,
yet the only cells destroyed were the ones
that might make him hard— he was soft now
like dandelion wisp drenched in twilight glow.

We were a three-day lockup, maybe a week,
and they brought him to us spilling nonstop gibberish,
after he had thrown a rock at the Berkeley police.
This escaped his memory as effortlessly
as Houdini slipping out of simple manacles.
One moment he was a chattering jay chick
with clipped wings, hopping from room to room,
pining for sky, singing chirpy backup to our frontline blues…

next he was a puppy with a splinter in his brain,
trembling with fright at loud noises, moaning
like a cavern on a windswept mountain,
when we broke it to him that he might be
forced to spend time in the Santa Rita jail.

We became his society for prevention of cruelty to crazies;
we adopted him, broke protocol, kept him for months,
until the law pried him from our hands, ruled he must be jailed,
for a crime he did not remember, where no one was harmed.

We pled before judges for dozens of weeks:
the closeted chief psychiatrist first,
the I've-seen-it-all-don't-bother-me head nurse,
the whole cuckoo's nest came together trying to save him.

They came for him late one afternoon,
cuffed him in the day room. He was calm,
gave us a quiet smile before the door
closed behind him.

A contagion of dread spread through us
like plague through a medieval town.
We knew—as we knew the moon
would magnet the tides that night,
and the sun roar in tomorrow's sky,
mirrored in rivers never forgetting
their way to the seas—
that this wobbly faun would not last
in the dark forest of the iron trees.

Tripping Out

To fathom hell or soar angelic
Just take a pinch of psychedelic.
> —Humphrey Osmond, the man who coined the term "psychedelic"
> (along with Aldous Huxley)

The scent of flower-filled trees in February
bulldozes her back to a time just nine months after
her first and secret lover has committed suicide.
She doesn't plan to eat the psilocybin alone,
it just works out that way; her guide can't come,
and she can't wait. It's nineteen-seventy,
the height of the evangelism and her virgin time,
but she is Lucy underground, nowhere near the sky,
trying to lift from beneath a bin of coal
shoveled into her mind.

There are bad moments: she is certain
Kathryn, who is flying in that night,
has just died in a plane crash.
As she rides her bicycle home,
the asphalt erupts in blood puddle potholes,
and everyone she passes knows she's lit,
sees the purple glow around her face and hands.
She is sure she has just made it inside her gate
seconds before being arrested.

Back in the safety of her own yard,
she gazes into the soul of an acacia blossom,
listens to its yellow siren call
to climb inside its core, chalk truths
across the vibrant blueboard sky.
These sun-soaked early spring caterpillar blooms
crawl their Day-Glo colors across the gray folds of her life,
shape shift to sparklers setting time on fire,

burn down trouble, whisper in her ear:
you must do the thing you think you cannot do,
mushroom explosion pressing coal to diamond.

At dusk, a doe and her faun nuzzle
in the neon grass outside her glass back door.

Tulipa humilis

Hey, my hands are dizzy.
        —from *Sleeping Where I Fall*, Peter Coyote

A dozen hot pink tulips burst skyward
in the breezeless air of the room—
helium balloons
on taut, green, leafy strings.

Anchored in a cobalt blue goblet,
they descant sweeping colorpraise:
notes of soprano cerise reach
higher and higher, kissing the ceiling,
striving to leak into clouds,
peach them.

Bless the Godfathers, Part 1

Do good. Be kind. Reach out.
    —Grace Yarbrough Clarke, great-granddaughter of Augusta, Georgia,
    Mayor William Bell

for James Brown, 1933–2006

The only two white boys in the Bell Auditorium
in Augusta, Georgia, 1964, they learned
the silky, syncopated moves of The Temptations
lifting Smokey's "My Girl" to the top of the charts.
They watched Dionne walk on by,
and Diana and her Supremes
belt out "Baby Love," and "Come See About Me."
And all through these nights, kind brothers
would come to them one by one,
offer to shelter them, shield them,
if anyone gave them a hard time.

They were fifteen,
and if my mother had known they were
drinking and learning the mashed potatoes
up close and personal from the master,
James Brown... and his Famous Flames,
inside those *Chitlin' Circuit* extravaganzas,
it might have thrown her over the precipice
of her newly-tenuous life.

Years later, when James was famous
even to the whites in his home town,
he sang happy birthday
to our beloved cousin, Tru,
in the Green Jacket Restaurant
near the Augusta National.
She blessed his heart

in a red-faced drawl with her head down,
hiding a Moon River-wide smile.

Yes, that hometown James Brown,
Godfather of Soul,
may well have soul-saved my bro
in those chaotic days
of Freedom Summer, Ruby Bridges,
days of Medgar Evers, JF and ML K leaving,
days of our parents' shattering divorce.

First Anniversary (Bless the Godfathers, Part 2)

for Alexander (Sasha) Shulgin, 1925-2014

Maybe it was Sasha Shulgin who saved my life in '70,
that first anniversary summer of my first lover's death.
Timothy Leary called him one of the twentieth century's
most important scientists, after all.

After failure with razors, pills, gas,
I grasped at a plan that seemed sure,
filled me with relief, gave me a strange, new happiness.
The sound of my own laughter pleased me for days,
and my friends noticed the uplift.
Five days into the ten-day waiting period,
this hot air balloon crashed, left me stranded
in an even more desolate landscape,
suffering severe dehydration of meaning,
not eating, sleeping, speaking,
guilty, humiliated by my own breathing.
Kathryn made me go with her to give the bullets back.

My friends urged me onto a plane to Atlanta
and I sat with Jerry, Lenora, Kathryn,
in Kathryn's tiny, music-filled living room,
swallowing MDMA with them,
having no idea what it was—Summer of Shulgin,
saturated with Sweet Baby James Taylor
and Natural Woman Carole King.

I was in love with all three of them by the end of the night:
Flaming Jerry, Bi Kathryn, Lesbian Lenora.
I swore allegiance to them each for life over that summer—
holy oxytocin, holy Carson McCullers' *we of me.*

Dear Sasha, Godfather of Ecstasy,
thank you for gifting us all MDMA
with no fanfare, no legal fight,
for melting my icy, dangerous snowpack,
for helping send streams of meaning
trickling back across my mindscape.

Your gift transformed me
from driving, death-wish-programmed-missile
to a chemistry of limerance. I lifted into love
with the three people sitting next to me, no conditions.
And the death drive did not strike again for over ten years.

The Call of the West

We are homesick most for the places we have never known.
—Carson McCullers

White fingers of fog grasp the bridge
as if to lift it from its moorings
along the headlands of Marin and San Francisco—
the strait named Golden Gate, once home of the Ohlone,
place where white, shark-fin sails
slice the water's blues and grays, and in the distance,
a miles-long, hump-backed whale of thick mist
rolls over hills beneath which humans teem like krill.

In salty air fog horns keen outside walls
where poets lift their voices over beer
sitting next to gas log fireplaces,
and sweethearts hear symphonies
after fragrant, wine-splashed meals,
where cold winds of street canyons carry sounds
of homeless pleading for coins and kindness
between raw coughs and schizophrenic outbursts,
as they stand in line for meals at Glide and St. Anthony's;
where Monterey cypresses green a golden park,
where bullets suddenly rip the air, where gays have married.

Up close, where fog chills or sunbeams heat its soft winds,
this people-plashed cove at the edge of creation
holds all colors, all stripes, all ages, all tongues
in its tender St. Francis embrace, its unconditional hippie hug.

Kaliflower Commune

Take notice, That England is not a Free People till the Poor that have no land have a free allowance to dig and labor the Commons, and so live as comfortably as the Land Lords that live in their Inclosures.
—The Diggers' Manifesto, 1649

On Clayton Street at Oak,
six of us shared a house
and a cat named Martha My Dear.
The Haight-Ashbury Free Clinic
was our next block neighbor.
We ate together, lit menorahs,
decorated Christmas trees,
and packed for Redwood forest
camping trips above the Russian River,
stopping to visit
deeded-to-God Morning Star Ranch
as we drove back home.
I still see Eddie's smile-wide face
rushing into our Victorian's foyer
holding up the released-that-day
Joni Mitchell *Blue* album.

Two years later, inside a three-story
building on Arguello Street,
I lived with lesbians in a middle flat,
egg salad between
top and bottom floors
of gay boy rye bread.

The Mime Troupe/Diggers
lit the Haight on fire in '67.
Their first Human Be-In in January
flamed into The Summer of Love,
then roared as a coffin-burning funeral pyre—

The Death of the Hippie, by October.
The wizards of this Oz
were signaling everyone to go back home by then.
Forget San Francisco and flowers in your hair,
Sgt. Pepper, and the Dead—
stay in Muskogee and Cincinnati.
The city was drowning in lost souls.

When I arrived in '69, I did not leave.
I knew something was happening—
an upbeat social earthquake
that made it safe to hitchhike…
and there were tight and fly-by-night
families of us living together everywhere.

Concentric ripples of the Digger sea change
lapped at our doors, touched us each week,
as a delivery of organic vegetables—
like a sacrament, and absolutely free.
And tucked inside the food box,
a wafer of graceful calligraphy
laced with psychedelic spirit art.
Kaliflower Commune ministered to
three hundred households of us.

By the early seventies, just before the drug war began,
the Digger/Free spirit of '67 still reached down into us
straight from 1640s England, from a rag tag group of poor
who had few tools back then to right the inequities of their time.
These Diggers fought with farming skills,
growing food on The Commons to share freely with all.

Most of us knew nothing about any of that
in our communal rooming houses,
but something in the air helped us trust
and have psychic wall-busting fun with one another.

This shiny, new, electric kool-aid tribal world
made us feel we had sprouted
hope-feathered wings that kept us hovering just above
all the things that wanted to bring us down.

Let thousands of fingers snap
in deafening beatnik ovation—
for Kaliflower, those ripped-jean angels.
They served us stories and veggie communion,
drew a vision-rich circle around
our Sancho Panza remnants.

III

Utopian Eyes

I play the radio and moon about...and dream of Utopias...
—Zelda Fitzgerald

The past history of the Oneida Community is at least secure....
The truth is, all the world will one day see and acknowledge,
that they have... been... social architects...
whose experiments and discoveries they sincerely
believed would prove of value to mankind.
—Harriet Noyes Skinner, Oneida Community member 1848-1880,
sister of John Humphrey Noyes

One of the mixed blessings of being twenty and twenty-one and even
twenty-three is the conviction that nothing like this, all evidence to the
contrary notwithstanding, has ever happened to anyone before.
—Joan Didion, *Slouching Towards Bethlehem*

All animals are equal, but some animals are more equal than others.
—George Orwell, *Animal Farm*

The Tangerine Submarine, Part 1

Jealousy is a disease, love is a healthy condition…one emotion hardly leaves room for the other.
 —Robert Heinlein, *Stranger in a Strange Land*

I escape the psych ward
that drew me to the Haight
for my second-ever nursing job,
rescued from a barely masked,
black, quicksand depression
by a gallant psych tech/artist
inviting me to live with him
in his tumbledown cabin in Forest Knolls.
We take turns as each other's guides
in separate mescaline trips.
I come out; he relives age five
as *kindertransport* orphan
losing everything but his life.

I move into a wacky household—
three lesbians and one salacious straight guy—
then meet the hippie version
of what Hollywood later turns
into *Bob, Carol, Ted, and Alice,*
a drop-out quadruple living together
using a *balanced rotational sleeping schedule.*
I am still bush-league human being, too green
to know that group-think three letter names
should ring alarm bells, so I don't run
when Vee, Aya, Eli, and Zig greet me,
and a fistful of other wandering souls,
with stories, art, guitar, visions
of California-going-global secular kibbutzim.
Like a rock band, they've named themselves!
and I can't believe my luck in discovering
The Tangerine Submarine.

It's early '70s and America is filled
with cross-country hitchhikers
climbing into pot-hazed
VW vans truckin' West,
tie-dyed curtains sliding open and closed
along their side and back windows.

Seekers, hopers, droppers, dopers
rent apartments, Victorian flats,
live together sharing expenses
and, in this case, more than that.

I have stumbled onto this winsome foursome
through my free university class, *Finding a Way Out*,
where they tell us we should dumpster dive
and learn to live with less.
A fellow student says she's met a group
that's *livin' the dream*, idealists trying to do
important, cool, farout things.

I circle with them week after week
at the Excelsior library's meeting room,
and they become a rhythm in my life,
until I am wholly entwined
in the dream tapestry they've woven,
from colorful, quixotic plans,
a *cri de coeur* against a *brave new world*.

We are *strangers in a strange land*,
rowing toward *Island*,
ecovillas and superfamilies
dancing in our heads,
hippie free love melting into
polyfidelity and village-wide parenting.

Tripmates

We behaved with both arrogance and naïveté, assuming that we were
leading the way to a future of our own design.
　　　—Peter Coyote, *Sleeping Where I Fall*

It begins with a chiseled young guitarist
and a World War II Air Force vet,
survivor of hell in the Philippines.
The guitarist has kicked an addiction,
and the vet is a blown mind who has tried
to build a lasting community
eleven different times,
once as expatriate in Dominica
(where Timothy Leary comes to join him,
just before they are each expelled from the island).
These two New Yorkers, the younger Italian in heritage,
the elder Jewish with Ukrainian roots, argue—
about whether the red on the top of the spaghetti
is gravy or sauce.

The older one seems a bit eccentric, but sparks
crackle from his brain like a current of electricity,
and fit the tenor of these times:
this lifestyle could catch on like McDonald's
and help save our planet from dying.

Vee, a young artist, shows up from New York,
after hitching a ride to the West with her parents.
Her comic strip sketches our lives like a diary.
(Twenty-eight years later, her father will win
the Nobel Prize in Medicine.)

Vee invites Aya, her feisty former high school pal.
Aya ditches her plan for college, hitches to the Haight.
These four become, by '72, a fidelitous family
sharing a flat on Shrader Street.

Note a Cowardly Lesbian on this Yellow Brick Road,
desperate for meaning and a place to belong.
She yields to her phobia, returns to *I'm bi,*
abandons a crucial strand of her self
for life in this heterocentric tribe.

An end-of-service Peace Corps vet
floats back, driftwood, to America's shores.
Pep is dazed and lost and seeking and joins
after teaching three years in a village in The Gambia.
Pep hails from New Jersey, as well as Liv,
aspiring spiritual counselor, our lyrical songsmith.

Meet Texan Ren, shot put champion uncrowned,
protesting this sexism in a hippie headband
at the school auditorium where she gets no award,
no satisfaction—girl thwarted in pre-Title IX times
escaping West for a feminist life.

Here's Fre, ex-Catholic from the Redneck Riviera—
she's the *red-haired girl in the Chevrolet*
vamping through Billy Joel's "Keeping the Faith,"
leaving her Blue Angel heartthrobs behind
for adventure on the continent's other side.
The closeted psych nurse from Georgia
is part of this Red State Runaways crew,
and a silver-tongued Reb from North Carolina—
who gets lost in drugs for a time,
after The Disillusionment.

Chef-ster, poli-scientist, punkster, poet—
all straight outta' Philly and to the Left Coast.
(*Tzaddik* we call punkster Taj at the end.
She pushes with humor against Eli's bullying,
gently defuses his storm cloud moodiness.
As hypocrisy smothers our esprit like mold,
she is first string midwife for the birth of *it's over.*)

We are *shiksa* goddess and *shayna maidel*,
Far Rockaway Ashkenazi, Red Bank Episcopalian,
kibbutz lovers, believers in nada,
admirers of Jesus, followers of Buddha,
high school dropouts, a UPenn grad.
We're artists, a novelist, psychology lovers,
ex-Christians, a mimic, a street corner busker.
We are tech wizards and libertarians,
and several excellent cooks.

One is heiress to a national food fortune—
disinherited by her family for joining us.
A relative of the shooter of Milk and Moscone
is one of us on that painful day.

Two Vietnam vets with bandaged psyches,
pummeled by the metal knuckles of war,
stumble upon us a few years ahead
of three bigotry-bruised African Americans.
Several of us, both female and male,
were criminally abused as small children.

A graceful German-American woman,
raised by Nazi-traumatized parents,
finds us after our children are born.
Her father shook hands with Hitler
as a small, uncomprehending boy.
Zen loves and cares for the children
with the devotion of Maria von Trapp.

The word *utopia* raises last wild hopes
inside the closeted suicidal.
Two, of a handful of these troubled ones,
leave our psych ward run by the inmates,
lose their battles with The Pale Rider.

We are refugees from a fifties famine of soul,
auditioning for the part of seventies hippies.
We are Lewis and Clarks and Vasco de Gamas
in Birkenstocks, tie-dyes, and peace sign pajamas,
seeking meaning through Mitty-esque visions,
many of us dragging old traumas behind.

We believe in the extrovert with Santa Claus hair,
this Eli, Einstein of communal dynamics.
He's raised his flag on a brand new shore,
setting up camp for his twelfth time.
His genes are rich in the oil of resilience.

We invite all seekers to our roaring hearth
with words as our only sentries.
We are warm and snug and as confident as Columbus,
that we've found the psychic East Indies.

The University of Utopia

The Tree of Understanding, dazzlingly straight and simple,
Sprouts by the spring called Now I Get It.
  —Wislawa Szymborska, "Utopia"

Acacia Glaziers now rents the store on Frederick Street,
the one with the plate glass window
above which we hung Vee's hand-painted shingle—
University of Utopia.

We invited the curious to come
with ads in our hip happy paper,
sprinkling those ads between hundreds more
from shopkeepers all over town—
Alex Holcombe's Jewelry store
on the corner of Haight and Ashbury,
or Harvey Milk's activist hive, Castro Camera.

People walking through the door did not know
they might need protective gear.
As they came to rap about changing the world
through building benevolent community,
they faced a swarm of intimate quizzing
that left them startled and defensive:
Are you monogamous or non-monogamous?
as they sipped their peppermint tea.

Most curious, searching souls
sputtered at our mosquito bite suddenness.
The secure among them had fun
talking ecology and new kinds of families,
until we kept on about unconscious motives
and straightsville conditioning—
You don't care about saving the planet...
you just wanna' get married in a church!

Yes, we needed to screen the non-serious,
but we did it with twisted Transactional Analysis—
I'm okay, you're a jerk.

People listened, laughed, wept, fled, some stormed away.
The wisest stood up to our tactless gropes.
The ring of Lost Children who survived all these games—
second star to the right and straight on till morning.

Vision with a Business

Do you want to sell sugared water for the rest of your life?
Or do you want to come with me and change the world?
        —Steve Jobs, recruiting CEO John Sculley from Pepsi to Apple in 1983

In 1984, Apple paints IBM as Big Brother
in a radical ad that runs during the Super Bowl.
Americans watch a blond, athletic woman in red shorts
stormed by menacing, riot-geared troopers.
She races past lines of ash-gray robes, soulless slaves
robot-trudging to seats in a monochrome assembly hall.
She gazelles ahead of the leaded troops,
strides up the hall's central aisle.
She swings her arm in a circle
in the perfect form of a discus thrower,
but instead lets go of a sledgehammer
that tears through the air like a missile, exploding
a wall-high dystopian face droning propaganda.
Seventy-two thousand Americans
buy a Mac by May of that year.

A few seasons beyond this iconic ad,
a swirl of reporters surges
around the man Steve Jobs has tapped
as he moves from one conference room to another,
announcing a project between Apple and Novell.

At this conference I sidekick Aya,
my fifteen-year-vintage commune sister,
watch her uncork her champagne chutzpah.
I witness as she bobs through waves of men,
landing like a breathless Olympian,
right in front and fully in charge
of John Sculley's attention.

As Aya speaks, the throngs of suited men
become scenery on the sidelines of her stage.
As if she has delivered an urgent telegram,
John Sculley reacts to her on the spot.
Call Gordon, he tells her as everything stops.
He flashes a card from his breast pocket—gold medal.

The waves close around him again;
the river of reporters and businessmen
reanimate, flow on to the sea of people
waiting in the next microphoned room,
and our utopian community soon becomes
the thirty-third-fastest-growing company in America.
A vision with a business we said.

After years of all-nighters prepping Macs
for NASA, Pac Bell, Pacific Gas & Electric,
and creating animation for companies
trying to sell to the Jet Propulsion Lab,
our vision with a business collapses—
economic and emotional bankruptcy.
The business that ate the vision we say
but really it was just a catalyst.

At the end of last year, Apple was worth
seven hundred billion dollars, and sold
its two-hundred-and-fifty-millionth Mac,
its five-hundred-millionth iPhone,

while we dust our musty old papers and ephemera
for a college that holds collections like this
from The Shakers and Oneida.

14th Anniversary (1983)

Donna Summer's "She Works Hard for the Money"
has just hit the top of the charts.
In our hippie, space gypsy garb,
a vanload of us from the commune,
drives to the out-of-doors Concord Pavilion
to see her perform.

On the cover of the album, Donna
dresses as a waitress in a pink uniform,
honoring a real-life, low-wage
working woman, Onetta.
Something about this flashy pop star
creating an Anthem for the Common Woman,
reaches deep inside me, unlocks a long-locked door.

She works hard for the money,
so hard for it honey.
She works hard for the money,
so you better treat her right—
wrapped in a driving rhythm,
tied with a silk ribbon of melody.

On a blanket in the grass
this mild July evening,
beneath a canopy of star lace,
a lead-heavy mantle of guilt and grief
falls across my shoulders, sinks me
into my own private Okefenokee.

Sting speaks
for my long-dead first lover—
Every breath you take
Every smile you fake...
I'll be watching you.

A sentencing—I am guilty—
her suicide my murder by omission.
The court appoints me executioner,
leaving me white-knuckled driving across bridges,
fighting the pull of their edges.

As I scrawl *despicable thing to do to our kids*
in the note to explain my leaving to my friends,
that line thickens into a wild vine
and I grasp it with both hands, pull my life
out of the sucking quicksand
into a howling wind of shame.

After weeks of life narrated by Kafka,
I order my friends into round-the-clock watch.
In shock, they listen as if I am Eisenhower,
ordering them to the beaches of Normandy.

Fre trails me to the bathroom for many weeks,
in vigilant, loving overkill,
long after I've returned to the world of the living.
Vee becomes hawkeyed manager
of me and of the children.
Aya is gobsmacked and tearful.
Punkster Taj
who hacked "Imagine" into protest poem—
imagine no possessions
cuz you sure ain't gonna get mine—
taps her Mariana Trench-deep
empathic pool of intuition,
and in the living room of friendship,
offers cool compresses of compassion,
for many months, against my *fever 103*
(foreshadowing her career-to-come as therapist).

Psychiatrists, meds, communal caring
lift me from this swamp of twisted cypresses
draped in a Spanish moss of old trauma.

I come out. I go back in,
not strong enough for years to be my queer self
or understand another strand of this breakdown—
the future—the egg of *us*
slowly starting to crack as we enter
our second decade of community.

Anchor

> *My mind's not right.*
> —Robert Lowell, "The Skunk Hour"

I do not have the energy to brush my teeth,
cannot hold the kite string of communication.
Characters on TV are odd, deep sea creatures,
while live people send me scurrying under rocks,
a frightened lizard.
I cannot read, yet every detail of
"Serotonin Levels in the Brains of Violent Suicides"
penetrates the haze, electrifies it.

As my ego ticks like a dying battery-run clock,
and I have trouble lifting a fork, putting on socks,
as my wispy self clings to a cliff's edge by fingertips,
my ghost heart racing above the river Lethe,
I grab the dangling rope that circles the granite boulder
of this *American Journal of Psychobiology* article,
hold on, praying, at last, for a different kind of courage.

Death Control Pills (Vintage 1980s)

fluoxetine's amphetamine,
a lean and hungry lift;
nortriptyline is snorazine,
with *sleep* supplanting *death*.

the choice is cheerful cheetah,
against sleep-happy sloth;
gazelle with failed libidah,
versus cumless moth.

it's sex and one half does, the other…
doesn't it seem a crime?
to forfeit joy beneath the covers
for the right to toast *l'chaim*!

The Tangerine Submarine, Part 2

For all its charms, the island is uninhabited…
all you can do here is leave
and plunge…
Into unfathomable life.
— Wislawa Szymborska, "Utopia"

We find ourselves in *Psychology Today*
and on *The Phil Donahue Show*;
social scientists study how we hang out,
write papers and teach courses on us.
We coin a word we say means
the opposite of jealousy,
empathy that rises
when those you love and trust,
love and sleep with one another.
We seem to feel this *compersion* for years,
before it slowly leaks away,
and our great communal tangerine balloon deflates.

We are a bell bottomed tribe
in a skin tight leather pants world,
eerily Oneida-esque utopians,
sixteen of us raising two pre-teenage girls,
and headed for, after twenty years,
spectacular poly-divorce.

Aerie

Unshakable Confidence towers over the valley.
Its peak offers an excellent view of the Essence of Things.
    — Wislawa Szymborska, "Utopia"

We crawled into the nest of his delusions,
bright-colored, wispy feathers of fantasy
woven smoothly into gray twig strands
of reality.

Baby chicks of the sixties,
we huddled with a papa loon—
young, tuneful birds, we flew,
but only near our own cliff side.
In time we gave birth
to chicks of our own.

We thought we were eagles,
cocksure that all the world
would see our majesty

until the rains came
washing wisp, feathers,
drenched coots
down the mountainside—
into a forest stream—
bobbing, crashing
over tree limbs, boulders,
toward the open sea.

Haight Garden

...the crack in the teacup opens
a lane to the land of the dead.
       —W.H. Auden

fallen camellias lie along the broken walkway,
behind the house that held communal hopes
for a score of years

year one is fun, fun, fun; I climb in the back
with my head in the clouds and I'm gone

after a rain, waxy, bronze blossoms
balance wet jewels on their tongues

they never take Lucy's diamonds,
they are high on saving the world

chocolate camellias that yesterday
crackled underfoot,
surrender to rain drops and fog,
dissolve into silence

year two: Fin spills from the top of the Hilton
almost takes a taxi driver with her

beneath the deep pink of the mother camellia bush,
a lawn of baby's breath—
duvet of green with coral confetti
sprinkled by flowering quince

they have two children by year eight

in the twilight, wild onions fly yellow furled flags
full mast above overgrown grass

they spurn jealousy, coin its antonym, compersion,
share lovers for years

Tibetan magnolias that burst
onto bare limbs in winter,
hold on in remnants,
like white silk rags
torn and tied onto branches
now mobbed with green

we fall through a hole in our flag

callas trumpet
from their sentry lines
against the weather-beaten back fence
that sheds splinters if you touch it

we tried in our way to break free

with the birth of its tender flowers,
the hawthorn carries a faint fragrance of sea

in year fifteen, D. sails
off the Golden Gate Bridge

in the distance a street car rumbles by,
a foghorn mourns

this backyard is home
of a belly up utopia

along the west fence, two evergreen saplings
need transplanting beyond this place

the two adult children are making a difference
in this world they've been planted in

passionflowers, scarlet stars
with broad rays and gold centers,
vine into a willow,
beam down on this garden
from the northside neighbor's yard

good evening, starshine

the rose bushes no longer give roses
the bamboo has died

even though it all went wrong,
nothing on our tongues but hallelujah

and the only gardening here now,
in this overgrown Eden,
is a plucking of the dead
and dying camellias,
rusty blooms that drop beneath
wind-kissed buds,
crimson, incandescent
in the San Francisco sun.

Morning

for Fin

I have not yet arrived home where your note
lies inside its sealed envelope on the kitchen table.
I am waking to deer nibbling, with cocked ears,
on the spring green hills of Mt. Diablo. The sun
is warm on my face for a while before I open
my eyes to those deer, and behind them pastel clouds
slowly blazing to white against the oxygen-rich blue
sweep of the morning sky. I am not thinking of you
now, but I will. It is just past dawn— hours before
Bill and I will go home to be with you again, you
with your harlequin hair, your scimitar grin. I have not
yet driven across the bridge back into the city at dusk,
where downtown buildings begin to light
like evening stars. It is before I climb the stairs to home
with camping gear and wonder for the first time
where you are. Before the note or the call to the morgue
when they say *no*, put me on hold then sharply,
after a long time, say *yes* they have a Jane Doe
from the top of the Hilton. We have not yet driven
down to the refrigerated room where the man
who learned we weren't family explained
that you split, nearly hit the driver of a taxi
as he stepped out of his cab at Ellis and Taylor.
It is not yet the time when the numbness took hold,
when the man in the lab coat pulled back the sheet,
showed us your egg shell face, bloodless, no trace
of mirth. No, this moment is not yet here. I am still
running in the warm air along the deer traces
brushed by budding branches of April trees.

Vigil

for Reb

Your brain dusted with methamphetamine
makes your foot tattoo the floor
as you tell me about your father's final days.
After the morphine stopped doing all it should,
you sat next to him in the car, drove him
through the North Carolina woods.
You pulled over to hold him sometimes
as he saturated his pain with whiskey and regret.
You drove him past tobacco fields
where he was born, where he was about to die.
This and all the griefs of your life
have begun to grow malignantly,
eating the best parts of your mind.
Helpless beside you as you try to
push your pain out of reach between the lines,
I break into your stream of words and ask
if you would like to take a drive.

West Wind

for Eli

Kerista is the only thing happening.
  —Allen Ginsberg, cited in "The New Bohemians,"
  New York City, 1956

The writing is intoxicating and irresistible....The creature you find in Speak
Memory *is rare enough to be zoo-worthy....[an] oddly bejeweled skull....*
[His] relationships, apart from his magical atmosphere... fail to meet many
measures ... If we weren't so in love with him, we might cringe from him.
  —Mary Karr, (*The Art of Memoir*) on Nabakov's memoir,
  Speak Memory

His breath is zephyr, ebbing,
as sunlight floods the blue sky
of his final morning,
this John Humphrey Noyes
of the twentieth century,
titanic man who bragged his way
toward a great sinking,
narcissistic Moses who never made it
to The Promised Land, prophet born
of a boy cowering on a ship's deck
waiting for a fiery death by kamikaze,
boy who is forced to kill or be killed in the Philippines,
who takes home a bronze star from those palm trees,
then parachutes into the Coney Island of his mind.

He cannot sell encyclopedias any more after this,
or keep the Cozy Tavern he has bought and run so well.
After a while he can only vend peace, amend Tevye's dream,
read stacks and stacks of good books all day long.

In '58 he walks into a police station
smoking a joint, holds interracial love-ins
striking against miscegenation laws.

When the cops bust his apartment, on a tip
that blacks and whites are carrying on inside,
everyone is naked, save his year-old daughter,
asleep in the next room wearing a diaper.

Confused, searching youth are iron filings
to his charged horseshoe magnet charm;
he is Great Oz, and, behind the curtain,
still the terrified boy listening to voices
saying he must save the world.
In 1956, the year of "Howl," Ginsberg digs
Eli's scene on the Lower East Side.
By '63, he headlines in the *Dominican Herald*,
as an expat hero who has burned his own hands
putting out fire engulfing an islander.
He invites beleaguered Leary to join him there.

This Eli, who may have lost *mispacha*
to Stalin's '30s *Holodomor*,
hatches a plan to end future wars—
peace easing in through ecovillas
of polyfide families and village-raised kids.
He dreams this as global community blueprint
one century beyond Oneida's end.

Mickey Rooney was his fifties swinger pal,
but in his vision Eli sees himself
as Andy Hardy in a hope opera
winning a Nobel Peace Prize—
not Don Quixote having a go at windmills.

As the years rolled on beyond
the post-commune cringing,
it became easier to love him
as aging, ill, troubled family member—
as the flawed, brilliant, wounded, and many times

surprise-party-kind-and-empathetic
Shakespearean character that he always was.

On this morning the young boy hiding inside is quiet,
does not tremble, breathes as if peace is near.
He has talked to his daughters by phone,
and Pep and I sing him his haunting, minor key
song written decades ago— siren call
to his magic Dominican mountain by the sea.

Mt. Fuji slowly obscures in the fog.
Butterfly folds back into chrysalis.
Frantic, manic hummingbird lands,
on a leafy, blossoming branch—
electrifying stillness.

Fire Season

for Loki

She is mad, mad with grief
as her carrot hair smolders—
mad at being forced off the road,
the one she knows will lead to reunion.
Mad with envy of easy breathers,
with disappointment at being plucked
before the harvest: the forgiveness,
the looking-back love that will ripen
in ten or twenty years.

As chemo burns her bald,
she is mad with fear
of what it means to be extinguishing.
Over time she burns into a tender
glowing coal, accepting it all, at thirty-nine,
bright-colored scarves wrapped around her head,
her bed surrounded by vases of cut flowers,
and peopled with friends
eating the takeout meals she can't take in.

This year she would be sixty,
and if she were here in the Haight again,
she would be feeding us all
in some version of our old community's
Tangerine Dragon Cooking School.

Every September,
the month her last flame flickered,
a roaring flame rekindles her spirit—
prison suit orange to holly berry crimson,
her favorite oil-rich eucalyptus trees explode,
re-enacting that blazing resistance—
her brilliant, driving, mad desire
to keep circling with us.

Dead Flowers

During her last week she would not let me
change the flowers clustered in vases
along her window seat. Her eyes could no longer
make out details the rest of us saw— brown edges
of the lemon roses, parchment leaves of the mums,
the sag of iris bursts, spent, past their prime.
Losing these, last in a lifetime of floral affection,
seemed too hard for her; so I left them
in their autumnal beauty, fingered the blue
delphinium flecks that snowed the sill,
watched her go in and out of consciousness
until she was no longer there.

A waxy hull remained, map of all the parts
of her that failed: broken, sallow skin stretched
translucent across her jutting collar bone;
infected, bitten nails; yeast-conquered throat
no longer trying to speak, name
those restless sensations of the last few hours
when we hovered helpless, stroking, holding,
trying to give the ease that only came
with the letting go. She was facing the flowers
when it was over— dark, dry blooms—
and though I tried again and again to close her eyes,
they kept opening.

Glass Bird

for Loki, for the whole coterie

The blue glass bird I gave you Christmas of '92
sparkles at the window
where it dangles on a leather thread.
You wore it to your last party
where you broke its mate and cried.

Today I found an entry
from our communal children's journal—
back thirteen years when we were
living in our Haight kibbutz,
sleeping with the same men, raising our kids.
Your entry was penned when my daughter was
nine months and twenty days old.

She was inconsolable when I began to work again.
She wanted me as I was leaving
for my midnight shift; I left her,
screaming and reaching, went off
in tears to care for the dying,
while you cuddled and quieted her,
let her have your milkless breast.

This morning my daughter, edging towards fourteen,
would have traded me for a puppy, or an old shoe maybe:
You worry about such insignificant things; it's irritating,
she wailed at me, and you're no comfort to her now.

I hold it to the sunlight— your blue glass bird of unhappiness.
After those eighteen post-commune months when we teamed
to try to help you beat the C that spread everywhere from your ovaries,
you gave it back wrapped inside a card
you'd scrawled on, two days before the end:
Thanks for the jammin' you wrote in purple ink.

My voice, a whispery echo, rises from the granite walls
of that universal grand canyon of sadness:

Soar, hippie sistermom,
jewel in the sparkling strand
of our earnest, yiddishe, rock 'n roll'n,
culty, passionate, self-important,
pie-eyed, lopsided, twentieth century string
of wounded, hope-drunk, utopian dreamers.
Soar, dear diamond, sparkle on…
and thanks for all the jammin.'

Polyfidelity

The term originated in the Kerista Village commune in San Francisco that practiced polyfidelity from 1971 to 1991.
   —Wikipedia (first entry in a "polyfidelity" Google search)

It's not what you don't know that gets you into trouble; it's what you know for certain that just ain't true.
   —Mark Twain

We laughed at the swingers,
told them they were simply changing partners
with a bit of dishonesty.
Usually, one half of the couple
was more into it than the other,
then one of them would fall hard
for an outside lover and want a divorce
(not an expansion)
and look down on swinging forever afterward.
We saw this over and over, but when
we tried pointing this out to the open couples,
who erroneously gravitated toward us,
no one wanted to hear it.

We were so full of ourselves, though,
so sure we had a sturdy new family structure
that would not become unstable like monogamy,
a new tribal unit for society
where no one would have to die alone!
So sure that we thought up generations of names,
building upon Oneida's *free love* redubbed *complex marriage*.
There was *non-promiscuous polygamy*,
wholesome non-monogamy, then *multi-fidelity*.
Finally we were *polyfides* living in *superfamilies*—
Best Friend Identity Clusters—
imagining our old age lying in hammocks of *ecovillas*
watching children of our children feeding hay to baby goats.

But the land we bought above Mendocino
had only lawn chairs and unstruck tents
by the time that we sold it.
A granddaddy rattlesnake
triggered the slithering away
from that *Ecotopian* fantasy.

If only it had been true
that our re-fashioned
Oneida complex marriage
had been something more sublime
than a colorful twenty-year swing
into the next intimacies of our lives.

Clark Kent Cult

In the early 1960s, Keristans…stretched the limits of a not-yet-very-permissive
society a long way…and portended what was coming with the hip communes.
— American Studies, Vol. 33, No. 2, Fall 1992, "The Roots of the
1960s Communal Revival," by Timothy Miller

We were not a chosen people; we
did not coerce, possess, unleash violence.
We did not trick with deceptive come-ons,
or submit to some higher god's will.
We did not think the world was ending
or stop those we met with from drinking or peeing,
or tell them we would help them *get clear.*
No, we didn't do any of that.
Our group's originator heard voices in the '50s—
you're the prophet of the next great religion of the world—
but he spun it lightly as a drug induced vision.
We made up our own humorous religion—
Black sister of Jesus as a comic strip character—
black lives matter wrapped in hippie poetry.

In many ways, we were not that different
from a run-of-the-mill dysfunctional family—
there were simply more springs that could sprong
in our larger, more complex dynamics.
But we held ourselves up, above monogamy,
certain we were improving on that structure's flaws.
So, like a preacher who is having an affair
while delivering a sermon on marital fidelity,
our foibles were fair game.

We drifted into the suburbs of cult,
each taking three-letter names,
and writing to our parents to let them know
we would no longer use the word *love* with them,
reserving it only for the spiritual.

When people left the entire scene,
they were "walking the plank" and "dead" to us.
We had thought-stopping language, jargon,
like *subconscious unresolved contradiction*
about whether you wanted to be where you were.
When a person's behavior elicited this *grope*,
there wasn't a reasonable way to deny it,
and you might be voted from your family
by partners fearful of this same fate
if they acted unsure or hesitated
after, usually, Eli brought this up.
No *momism or popism*, more culty language,
that made biological parents feel crazy.

We created concepts like *graceful distancing*
and peaceable *divide and regroup*, easing things off
when tensions arose, a no-fault backing away, without angst,
to see if you missed someone— drawing back close if you did.
We were each at the center of our own universe
of *concentric relationship rings*—
a transcendent idea for our group dynamics,
but too many times we played strange games
with these perfectly wonderful ideas.

We were egalitarian in basic ways that papered a hidden hierarchy.
If you weren't in the *Tangerine Submarine* family,
you were less-than, no matter how much we denied it.

Despite an underground drumbeat of dysfunction—
of verbal dominance and submission—
we had long, halcyon periods
of tranquility, art, scholarship, and deep affection.
We were in love with psychology, and Liv and I taught
a California-credentialed continuing ed course—
Utopian Psychology for nurses who loved it.

We were a mild-mannered, nerdy, Clark Kent cult,
not a Superman *Halle Bopp* or *Jonestown*.
We fashioned an iconoclast community
using the freedoms of the sexual revolution
that Eli helped spark in the early sixties.

We were thinkers and dreamers and non-jealous lovers,
flawed yet sincere in our tribal lab,
hoping to bring something good to the world.
If we did nothing more, perhaps we helped open
a few *polyamory* closet doors.

There is a baby to cherish with this bathwater toss—
spirit genes of the Shakers, New Harmony, Brook Farm,
of Plato, More, Fourier, Owen, and our not-identical Oneida twin.
Under certain conditions, humans do give birth
to these social, imperfect *objets d'art*
for scholars to amber and quietly gift
to scholars of the future.

Good Times

The commune is both our church and our mental hospital.
        —Article in *Good Times*, about the Good Times Collective, 1969-1972

It is easy in an aftermath
to look at all the ways you failed.
Putting down your former self
can be a strange and easy way of saving face.
But what about the good times
that came before the collapse?
Shouldn't those have a museum of their own
separate from the ticking off
of what and why and how it all went wrong?

The times were swelling with whitecaps of change.
The Good Times Collective, folding as we began,
ran radical images in their *Good Times* paper—
San Francisco's Coit Tower as a finger to *the man*,
First Bird of Spring gesture on their front page.
This writers' seedbed gave us Alice Waters
and her radically healthy Chez Panisse.

Our tribal good times shine decades later—
the camaraderie of the women sharing a room
on those Zero Nights of our Sleeping Cycle
(there were always more women than men),
or the tables we staffed in Golden Gate Park
for International Women's Day.
The Keep Abortion Legal chapter we began in '73.

Inviting Michael Hennessey to our Monday night dinner,
going door-to-door for him, helping him win his first election
in his 32-years as progressive sheriff of San Francisco.

Rallying in the Castro with Harvey and Dennis
against a proposition that would ban gay teachers—
and Tom Hayden and Jane Fonda showing up to help.
(Jane: *I was so happy when I was with Harvey.*)

Evenings of theater with skits and songs.
Aya's script "The Generation Rap."
Sam's deadpan acting that spoofed our foibles.
Ben's meticulous journal (alas, lost at the end).
Philly poet, Ana, and her *giggle bath*.
Liv's Indigo Girl-level songwriting gift—
rendering our city as *jeweled plate*.

Ren, our masterful mimic, becoming Shirley Temple,
dimpling and tummy-aching in that lollipop plane,
before gyrating and crooning just a moment later
as Elvis rockin' the jailhouse.
We'd howl and she'd transform into Janis
belting her *Mercedes Benz* blues;
then, blowing breathless birthday kisses,
she'd slink into Marilyn.

Also, Ren deadly serious, fully-clothed in a pool,
grabbing our one-year-old to her by diaper,
two seconds after her gleeful march
from earth and air into sparkly water.

Our women's harmonic singing group, *The Sleeping Schedule*.
Our punk band we dubbed *Sex Kült*.

The Storefront Classroom, Utopian Eyes,
Rockhead, The Node— our ever-evolving pubs.

Vee's *Far Out West* strip run at Rip Off Press,
home of those famous *Freak Brothers*.
The tongue-in-cheek birth in those comics

of a sneaker-clad Sister Kerista—
Black sibling of Jesus—
and her multicultural pantheon
of exotic goddesses and gods.

The huge attic in the Haight
where we partied with our friends,
in feathers and sequins, leathers and silk,
fishnet stockings and high heeled boots,
where we hung Vee's giant poster
for The Joan Jett Haight Ashbury Fan Club.
The backstage pass for three of us to meet her.

Those wall-to-wall sofas in the Lavender Room
where we gathered for delicious communal meals.
Watching movies together in our homemade theater
of risers, couches, and armchairs
in the back of our *University of Utopia*.

The all-commune trips to Harbin Springs;
backpacking in the High Country of Yosemite;
camping at Mt. Shasta; and whitewater rafting,
splashing down the American River.

Polyfidelity: An Alternative Lifestyle Without Jealousy?—
Israeli scientist Ayala Pines' research paper—
that led to an article in *Psychology Today*,
and CBS flying Vee, Liv, and Reb
to Cleveland for the *Donahue* show.

Our two girls' births in an Alternative Birth Center.
Sparrow Village, our children's flat
that we adults took turns living in,
mimicking the system of the Israeli kibbutzim.

Sixteen adults raising the children—
our own and the children of single mothers
who joined us throughout the years.
Montessori, Better Baby, Suzuki violin,
and the kids in our easy chair theater
performing as pilgrims, Santa Claus, Lincoln.

The children on the computer in the late eighties,
at ages eight and nine, instant-messaging us
to stop working into Friday evenings
and watch *Mary Poppins* or *Clue* with them.

Playing games with Synanon, dining at Delancy Street,
once meeting with members of the People's Temple
at Fillmore and Geary.

Santana's sister-in-law, Kitsaun,
feeding us meals and kindness
at Dipti Nivas on Church and Market,
a '70s and '80s vegetarian haven.
We traded space in our newspaper
for the privilege of eating in places like this.

Aya waiting tables at the Island Restaurant,
Dennis Peron's front for his pot shop
just a short flight of stairs above it.
Gay Dennis who sat so patiently with us
gently destroying our phobia.

Robert Anton Wilson dropping by
for one of our *Gestalt-O-Rama* evenings.
Listening to Allen Ginsberg read from *Howl*
at the University of San Francisco.
Hearing Timothy Leary speak
in our neighborhood *Other Café*
where we went to hear Bobcat Goldthwaite,
and Robin Williams before he was famous.

We were urban adult summer campers
who did not go home at the end of the summer,
marathon-watching old movie musicals
at the Avenue Theater in our early years' evenings—
An American in Paris, Singing in the Rain
inspiring us to take lessons in tap dancing
to mesmerize the community-curious
with our shuffle, ball, change brilliance.
Imagine and laugh, hippies trying to pull off
Hey kids, let's put on a show.

In this era of earnest, yet arrogant rebellion,
our bags of magic may have come up empty.
Yet sewn into seams, perhaps tiny seeds
of Fourier foresight, Owen compassion, kibbutz ideals,
of Digger action from the seventeenth century.
Liberté, égalité, sororité imperfect!
in our wildflower and weed-filled dream garden.

Decades on, we finger these seeds,
our own and those before our time.
We package them, stamp them *fragile* and *urgent,*
mail them down the road to the future,
folded inside yellowed newspapers
with radical, beseeching headlines—

Close the Jails   and   *Set Our Warriors Free*—

from the good people of the *Good Times.*

Ridgetop

*The post-fire bishop pines had an electric quality, as though some plugged-in
current was emanating from them, making bark and needles glow....*
—David Rains Wallace, 17 years after the Mt. Vision Fire at
Pt. Reyes National Seashore

for the Twelfth Kerista Commune Incarnation, San Francisco, 1971-1991

Charred bishop pine forest of our communal lives,
stark stubble against soft, tangerine sky.

Olympian mountain range, once jungle green
mantled in sun's gold scarves,

transformed through naiveté, negligence, revolt
into high desert of gray ash and charcoal.

Silhouettes of skeletal limbs and trunks
pock the hills like makeshift grave markers.

Two decades on, roaring chlorophyll
carpets the former bald and barren peaks.

Emerald needles of thriving seedlings now touch,
smother the ridgetop with life.

Years after explosive, fiery catastrophe,
birdsong encores over Valhalla.

Hearth

Come, come, whoever you are.
Wanderer, worshipper, lover of leaving.
It doesn't matter.
Ours is not a caravan of despair.
      —Rumi

This house is a character in the play, fat and jolly, arms open, embracing
familiar hobo souls who drift in from road trips and vision quests,
drawn by whiffs of warm cinnamon, or whispers of ghosts.

As I try to read and write, weave silky white space around me,
the house issues sudden invitations, then whistles in the wind,
lifts its window shades skyward as if it has not called out
to these wanderers searching for themselves.

This Haight-Ashbury home wears sweat pants and pajamas,
shuffles in sock feet, secretly stuffing people in its pockets.
I am simply the hearthkeeper handing tissues to the weepers,
feeding the love-hungry dreamers who ring the bell.

This stained-glass-window-wearing San Francisco shotgun flat
cradled the fires of a last century utopian community.
Hope and innocence haunt it.

The veterans know
a pilot light still burns at its center.
The telephone rings and its blue flame leaps
to crimson and gold.

IV

Children of the Dream

A person's a person, no matter how small.
—Dr. Seuss

Children begin by loving their parents;
as they grow older they judge them;
sometimes they forgive them.
—Oscar Wilde

To My Fourteen Southern Aunts and Uncles

—for our children

It isn't hard to see how I believed
that a covey, a bevy, a herd, a pack,
a posse, a passel of parents would be better,
given those hug-luscious summers
when as many as ten adults would take turns,
trot out finger steeples and finger people,
ride me on their shoulders, teach me
to catch throw-back bream with bamboo poles,
or show me how to crank the old Victrola in the barn
to ring out quavering, disembodied voices
from those half-inch-thick, spinning vinyl disks.
Those tribal summers left indelible tattoos
as we caught lightning bugs and dropped them into jars,
icepick holes punched in the tops,
then cuddled in laps in the abracadabra darkness,
watching those fireflies blink their fairy lights.

Oh, my dear uncles and aunts, surrogate moms and dads,
you who would point at my chest and say *what's that?*
then blubber my lips or thumb my nose when I looked down.
You, my ensemble cast of Great Depression-surviving kin,
tap dancing for me like Ginger and Fred, plucking guitars
like Hank Williams, wearing your Grand Ole Opry grins;
you and your bear hug clasp on life, your presence, your *élan vital*,
made me believe: *polyfidelity* would wrap our children
in a silken cocoon of *joie de vivre.*

Child

You must be there
beside her when she decides
she will parachute out of the plane,
and you'd better have double-checked
all of her equipment and explained to her
every nuance of those rip cords as well.
After the heart-stopping free fall, she
will drop like a rock, or her silk
will billow in the wind
then snap tight,
as she drifts
slowly

to

ground

Goddess Child *(1994)*

And you are still my daughter.
   —W.D. Snodgrass, *Heart's Needle*

I was the first one to snap a picture of you,
at one second old: your unusually beautiful
newborn face is preserved in portrait light
somewhere on slides (our parental mementos
are scattered, just like our once
community-entwined lives).

Our California kibbutz, your multiple parents,
are no more; you live alone now with your father,
but I know your story
from its gleam-in-the-eye beginnings,
your parents like the back of my hand.

Your first kiss, your first sip of beer,
right here under my roof
after our community exploded.

You're fifteen.
Here comes the future;
take into it what you've seen.

I am your goddess parent.
I am your friend.
I live on your sidelines.
I'll be there, kid,
as you race down youth's road
and rip that ribbon
into adulthood.

Children of the Dream

Love children especially, for they are ... like the angels; they live to soften and purify our hearts and to guide us.
　—Fyodor Dostoyevsky

I knock and turn the knob at the same time,
only to be reminded entering
my thirteen-year-old daughter's room,
that I am only going through the motions
of honoring her privacy, that I should
wait for her voice, her permission to come in:
this said matter-of-factly, eyes still on the TV.
You're right, I smile.
She and her sister (they share no genes,
only eleven years together in a communal family)
live together now only on weekends.
Bundled in rumpled blankets up to their arm pits,
cathode light flickers in their eyes, as they
peer from matching pillows on twin beds.

I bring blueberry pancakes soaked in syrup—
all is forgiven—they give me brief attention.
I get my own plate, and while they watch
the screen, I pretend to, but instead,
I think about them.

From birth they were the center of
sixteen adults' parental attention.
We edited their *Sesame Streets* for violence,
taught them to swim, flashed red
math dots and vocabulary words at them
before they were two. Home school,
camp, gymnastics, Suzuki violin—
we tried to think of everything
to nourish them, but before it was over,

sixteen business-harried parents relied on Vee
to orchestrate care, remind us of shifts at Sparrow.
Towards the end, sometimes they opened
their own cans of SpaghettiOs for dinner.

We were a tense and feckless superfamily by the end,
as time carried us from our utopian vision
to an explosion of our self-deprived lives.
We limped along hiding in overwork,
trying to deny we were moving
away from each other at the speed of light.
Toward the end, the soul of the happy, hippie
American kibbutz left the building, but we kept on,
trying to deny we'd gone past *Pollyanna*
into a soft-focus, flower child version of
Who's Afraid of Virginia Woolf—
inside our once jealousy-free lives.
None of us wanted to believe or touch
the creeping jade; we called it painless punk,
but it wasn't.

After twenty years, the marriage is over,
and here I am—Prozac-popping single mom
bringing blueberry pancakes
to the children of the dream,
praying time and tenderness will heal
any of their invisible scars.

The girls mumble thanks for the food,
don't take their eyes off the TV.
They are stumbling toward adolescence,
as I trip into midlife crisis—
and all our emotions, my friend, are wild
and blowin' in the wind.

Slumber Party

Two large pots of Kool-Aid
sit on top of a beach towel on the kitchen floor:
new teen fashion in dyeing hair.
Flowered cereal bowls with tiny lakes of milk
dot the counter. The oven is still on from
warming garlic bread. Wads of damp towels
rest like crescent cats asleep on kitchen chairs,
above mud footprints tracked in after
sneaking outside to the backyard for a smoke.
An empty pizza box sits on the table open,
back against the wall. Flat, tepid soda cans
sprout between piles of debris, like mushrooms.
Muscular rhythm of rap thrusts from the bedroom
where three class-of-ninety-seven girls lie
passed out from the intensity of adolescence.
As they dream their way toward tomorrow,
the radio slips into sixties soul.

Beside Your Self

as exceptional as laughter
you will strike fire,
that new thing!
    —Anne Sexton, "Little Girl, My String Bean, My Lovely Woman"

I sit beside you as you kerosene
your hurt and torch it,
as words fly out of your mouth
like riled wasps
smoked from a parchment nest,
and try to tell you,
without dampening or fueling
your flames, without getting burned,
that your fire, contained, is all right.
Protecting myself makes me
less than smooth: ballet dancer
in a fireproof beekeeper's suit.
On Wednesday you turn fifteen.

Natural High School

By commune's end, Reagan's dirty snow
had blanketed America's neighborhoods,
cracking fragile families, blizzarding in a new Jim Crow.
Colors—*norteños* red, *soreños* blue—
fought to the death on the same streets
where youth were making their way to schools.

When our high schoolers were late for class,
embracing one another in the hallways,
after news of rapes and deaths
of bystanders and friends, their teachers
sent them to the office, did not understand.

It took a village to honor the pleas of our teens
for a home school away from the ruptured trust
inside the public one they were attending.
Ben became our principal, as teacher
with the State cred to certify, legitimize
our home-school-within-the-local-public-high.

A handful of ex-communards built a buffer
around a tiny band of at-risk, school-misfit kids.
Liv taught English, calling for serious papers
on Shakespeare by Monday a.m.
Aya taught business math, Reb horticulture.
Jay laid out American History, and Gail
wrapped a cape of Women's Studies around them—
stories of sheroes' struggles and triumphs.
Gym was a karate class.

The savvy, compassionate counselor at their public school,
gave us one semester's credits after our students learned
and tested well. She encouraged us for months, but became ill.

A new principal, despite my pleas, despite
a call from my *San Francisco Chronicle* reporter friend,
denied our kids their graduation day.
We gave them artistically rendered diplomas
in a ceremony we held in a breathless meadow of Golden Gate Park.

These resilient young women went on to get their G.E.D.s.
Now B is in law school; C is a public defender.
Our youngest is a family medicine physician.
Our oldest is an exceptionally kind teacher,
operating an invisible Natural High
inside a very lucky public school.

White Girl Turns 21 in the Hood

When you're given a brilliant child you polish her and let her shine.
　　—Barbara Kingsolver

After your goddessmother, Aya,
gifts you a thousand dollars and you finish repairs,
boys drive by, trap your car in crossfire.
Over ghetto blaster rhythms rising from the street,
tires shriek, rubber smolders—engine thunder,
Colt lightning— bullets storm your car's body, just missing
synthetic vessels, metal heart.

The young women inside—
one visiting from Columbia—escape
without visible wounds.

Front passenger window and back windshield smash
into sleet-like heaps of splintered glass;
side mirror hit kaleidoscopes the reflection
of a nearby lone street light into myriad;
thumb-sized craters moonscape the trunk.

You puzzle, struggle— were you targeted,
activist living in The Bayview with your black boyfriend?—
decide the attack was random, gangs going at each other.

We repair the rear windshield with used glass—
University of Iowa decal still in place—
patch the bullet holes, paint this red car black,
half a month before your twenty-first birthday.

When people are oppressed,
they turn on each other like this you say,
sand and moisture in your voice
as twenty-one-going-on-forty battles

twenty-one-going-on-fifteen
in flickers across your face.

Two years later, Cuba
will gift you a scholarship to med school
for the promise of practice
in this kind of community, your briar patch.
Diving into this news, you will swim hard
from City College Spanish 101 to fluency,
visit your grandmother for the last time,
sell the old car, fly to Havana and its *Malecón*,
your new hood for years to come.

But tonight, with none of this in sight,
you celebrate your twenty-first year on earth
with a glass of sparkling wine,
and replace the *University of Iowa* decal
with one that reads *School of Life*.

Meditation from a Law-Breaking Visit to a Forbidden Island Nation

Landing on this Jewel of the Caribbean,
I look out onto the Great Blue River—
Hemingway's term of endearment—
for this island's layered
cerulean-sapphire-navy moat,
home of leaping marlin,
towering cumulus sculpture,
of makeshift leaky boats.
Its siren call to a northward Eden
leads through heartless sun,
through choppy waters
lit at night by tropical moon,
or sudden deadly lightning.
Over the wall of the *Malecón*,
beyond the sharks and flash squalls,
lies golden *Florida*,
and the uneasy freedom
of a foreign urban minefield.

Blue, white, red flag
snaps, stiffens in the wind
above *El Capitolio*,
above outrageous billboards
screaming *patria o muerte*
into the diesel-wrecked air
around a *jinetera*
hustling for the right to buy
empty, white bread
for her mother, for her child.
At night she dreams of sails,
smells salty sea air, unaware
of what it might corrode.

Blue, white, red feathers—
pajáro nacional
flashes its colors
like an unmoored kite
through the treetops
of the green *Sierra Maestra.*
Like the Taino who once lived here,
it sings its deep melodies,
unaware of its fast flight
toward extinction.
Even to save it,
humans may not
hold this creature close,
and all islanders know
why this caged bird
never sings.
They understand why
their beloved *tocororo*
always dies in captivity.

Notes:

The *Malecón*: a broad esplanade, roadway, and seawall which stretches for 8 kilometers along the coast in Havana, Cuba.

El Capitolio: the National Capitol Building, now a museum, in Havana.

Patria o muerte: homeland or death

Jinetera (from the Spanish word for a horse rider): the generic term given to prostitutes in Cuba.

Pajáro nacional: national bird. The *tocororo* is the national bird of Cuba.

Sierra Maestra: mountain range in Southwest Cuba (where Castro won the Revolution in 1959)

Taino people: indigenous inhabitants of Cuba devastated by colonialism, slavery, disease.

Gracias, Cuba

Beyond all your flaws,
you have given the world
over twenty-five thousand physicians
from eighty-four countries around the globe.

Your doctors flew into the aftermath
of the Indian Ocean tsunami,
into the aftershocks of the earthquakes
of Chile, Nicaragua, Peru, Java.
Your teams slogged into action
as mudslides in Venezuela
killed tens of thousands.

Your physicians were the first to arrive in Haiti
after its devastating earthquake in 2010,
our newly minted doctora-daughter
arriving in a later wave of this,
your Henry Reeve Brigade, army invading
countries across the planet, carrying weapons for
medical compassion— aid rejected by America
in the wake of Hurricane Katrina in New Orleans.

This Reeve Brigade— named
for an American doctor from Brooklyn
who fought in the first
War for Cuban Independence in the 1860s.
These Cuban docs rushed, lion-hearted,
into the fight against the invisible,
deadly ebola virus
in Liberia, Guinea, Sierra Leone.
The world honored them
as Nobel Peace Prize nominees in 2015.

Gracias, Cuba, tiny Caribbean country,
for devoting so much of your treasure and soul
to caring for earthlings living beyond
your sea-encircled borders.

And *gracias, Cuba*,
for gifting our daughter
(*yanqui, yuma, Americana*)
una madre Cubana llamada Amanda—
and, the degree of doctora.

The Kids are All Right

One is a poet-souled teacher
wise in the art of opening minds
of those with learning challenges.
She is an introvert,
a steady mama bear in her cave,
unless there is a threat to a cub,
her own or her daytime charges.
When she thought her principal
was causing harm, she left her cave,
plunging into job-risk danger.
In the public free-for-all
that heated from her speaking out,
she pled her case to the community
and the school board removed this boss
who could have just as easily
removed her from her cubs.

The other is a dreamer, an extrovert,
a friendly, loving wolf roaming the world
forming packs of family and friends.
One of her packs is thirty-six strong— she
and her co-residents in her Family Medicine program.
When the police shot and killed a young bipolar patient
receiving treatment in their E.R.,
this dreamer and her team, bled out a letter
to the mayor and the chief of police,
to their hospital, their union, the public,
pleading against guns in healing spaces,
urging mandatory Code Gold training,
a teaching of all involved in giving care
the skill of working together in humane harmony—
doctors, receptionists, security, janitors alike—
all, at once, wrapping psych emergency patients
in the safe medicine of understanding and de-escalation.

Whatever these two girls went through during their childhood days
as our commune flailed in a well of dysfunction,
only their memoirs will tell;
but as adults, they are lovers of *social justice*
(that idea given to humanity by the Jesuits in the 1800s),
practitioners of *tikkun olam*, the Hebrew concept
of repairing the world. These Gen X-ers might say
they are simply doing their jobs, but these two
phenomenal women (each in her own characteristic style)
are activist humans, making compassionate waves in their lives.

V

Mid-Life Kiss

We are so accustomed to disguise ourselves to others,
that in the end, we become disguised to ourselves.

—Francois de la Rochefoucauld

Dance, dance, for the figure is easy
The tune is catching and will not stop
Dance till the stars come down with the rafters
Dance, dance, dance, till you drop.

—W.H. Auden, from "Death's Echo"

30th Anniversary

(1999)

It's malarial, this fever of grief
that returns as faithfully as it leaves.

In good years it's easy to forget—
the cyclical nature eclipses;

yet, like a comet,
no matter how long the orbit,
it comes again;

you tremble, burn, take to bed
in an ague
of remembrance, regret.

Onset

Something in me vibrates to a dusky, dreamy smell of dying moons and shadows.
—Zelda Fitzgerald

When she goes from flesh and blood
to molecules of carborundum,
when taste of dandelion wisp
is in her mouth and on her lips,
when concentration evaporates,
memory is liquid, shapeless,
she aches for sleep;
when nothing pierces gloom—
not sharp wit or danger, not anger, not anything—
when all appetites are gone and there is no light source,
it is late, the air mephitic with doom.

But before tears come every day
as copious, steady tropical rain,
before low rumble of boulder
that would close her, alive,
inside a sepulcher,
there are clues, warnings;
fog devours a shoreline slowly.

As the shadowy black dog snarls
in a darkening forest,
crouches to pounce,
tear its teeth into her reason,
she arms,
more likely to win against in her fifties
what she lost to when she was seventeen.

Moonscape

The grief, when I finally contacted it
decades later, was black, tarry, hot,
like the yarrow-edged side roads
we walked barefoot in the summer.
　　—Diane Seuss ("Toad")

Body set upon by melancholia becomes
police state. Food is suspect. Armed guards
hold sleep at a border checkpoint.
Color fades into a crowd of protesters.
Concentration runs down a back alley,
blunders over a fence, escapes.

In time, there is a hustle of prisoner to launch pad,
an earthquake rumble, a flicker of sparks.
A death, a loss, some random helplessness
may have been the rocket fuel, but you have blasted off
to the not-quite planet, where you are lead feather
floating in grayscale silence, staring at barren crags
through the bell jar facemask of a cumbersome spacesuit.

There are no streets, no forests, only basaltic plains:
a Marsh of Decay, a Bay of Rain, of Roughness,
a Sea of Cold, of Storms, all dry volcanic afterlife,
even the crater called The Lake of Death.

This luminous white gold moon that used to thrill you in its fullness,
is dark, rusty dirt beneath your feet now, and you are drawn
to the siren beauty of its bleak, sand swept Sea of Tranquility,
treacherously named, where the curious weightlessness
of your boot-heavy steps makes you wonder if you really exist,
as you stare the two-hundred-thirty-nine-thousand miles
back toward the blue-green marble.

A voice says *start pills*,
and one morning there is
a refreshed waking from sleep,
a colorful view from a bay window, a breakfast to eat,
and ten thousand magenta pennies and tiny silk moons
spinning in the wind, drifting beneath cherry trees
and dancing onto the soft, red cobblestone street
that rolls like an ancient river
toward the earthy, fragrant eucalyptus acres
of this neighborhood's treasured canyon, Sutro Woods.
And in the evening, a pearl-white moonlight
licks the forest's newborn leaves.

Concentration returns from its life on the lam, and you read:
Helen Keller could feel moonlight on her face in the evening.

Mid-Life Kiss

Some of us think holding on makes us strong; but sometimes it is letting go.
—Hermann Hesse

soft startle of kiss cracks vessel
holding back tears; sorrow rises
swallows sun, moon, sky

tender, unexpected press
of womanlips on womanlips
brings polar darkness…
black, stormy grief… then
starlight

New Blooms in the Botanical Garden

Love makes your soul crawl out of its hiding place.
—Zora Neale Hurston

We came out
sitting on a wooden bench in the Redwood Grove
of Strybing Arboretum in Golden Gate Park,
to the amusement of our friends
who knew us only as starling sisters
who had slept with the same men
in a hetero-poly communal family
back in the seventies.

Our goddessdaughter, age nineteen,
walked in on us kissing.
Soon the cat would be out of the bag
playfully batting spilled beans across the floor.

So, on an April day in '98, on an already-planned walk
with our dear starling sister friends,
we declared our love—
beneath those majestic evergreens,
and beside an upstart army of sorrel
waving canary trumpets in the wind.

Shooting Scars

A scar is stronger than skin.
—Clarissa Pinkola Estes

Over the decades since the summer of '69,
invisible cicatrix have choked out reason
from time to time, transferring
proud flesh onto my body.

Up as the cheekbone ends,
on the right side of my face,
where the smile lines around the eyes radiate,
a wispy, white streak of raised skin
remains from a radiator-next-to-pillow burn
during the far away sleep of an overdose,
antidepressants at twenty-three.

On my left wrist, a line resembling white ink—
line once spilling yellow fatty tissue and blood,
line I stopped cutting into my own cadaver mid-job.
I put a Band-Aid on it, went to work—
psych nurse in charge of the acute ward.
I spent that day making sure
no one slit a wrist on my watch.

As I walk outside today,
the tops of the trees sway wildly in the wind,
while ivy, Virginia creeper, and cedar close to ground,
stand perfectly still, breathless.

My shoes bleed leaves
as I scrape them against the steps leading inside
from your red, gold, green back garden.

On this mid-October morning,
close to the arms of the Belgian forest,
the steadfast sun of your devotion rises,
gently eclipsing my constellations of scarlight.

Long Distance Love

Spin cycle of this time's visit—
no more waterfall rush
in this season of flush existence.

Soon we'll come to a sudden halt,
flattened against the circular wall
of our life together, we'll be hauled out
by the hand of fate, hung on separate lines
to dry— trying not to wrinkle inside—

clean, fragrant with love, waiting
to be taken up by life again, dreaming
of the next wet mingling.

Sparks

I am dancing, dancing earnestly to the Great Spirit,
And dance and dance til I can dance no more.
    —Potowatomi Chant

We move to the music,
relocate parts of ourselves
that have slipped out of joint,
beginning as sovereigns,
each taking to the floor alone,
until the notes are gale force,
thrusting us closer.

Earthy, mischievous smile
slides across your face
as you throb and sway toward me
like a sexy, African queen.
We are eye to lusty eye,
our hands lighting
like Monarch butterflies
on the eucalyptus trunk
of our dance-clasped bodies.

Molecules mingle, endorphins waltz—
I am lost in sensation of arrival.
We are dancing, dancing, dancing,
sparks light our faces.

Six Months In

You look to me for wisdom,
a way to make sense
of your sudden, new landscape
of same-sex attraction.

You don't know you're asking Crane's
Union soldier, Henry Fleming,
about his *red sickness of battle*, his flight,
abandoning his fellow tattered soldier
to die alone in the forest.

You don't know,
that with Birmingham and Stonewall
as distant, unbearable locations
far beyond the primitive shack
of my melancholic mind,
I watched my fellow nursing student, Sam,
jailed, simply for being who he was;
and Jerry, who loved opera, especially *Aida*,
deliberately decide to suicide by AIDS.

What will you do when you know
how I saved no one and nearly died myself,
how I can't guide you, except to tell you this?

Brave woman who heart hunted me,
let's forget wisdom… and party!
It *is* 1999! and we are in San Francisco!
Let's hit the dance floor,
draw our friends close— celebrate!

Still, in quiet moments I hear
the beat of an underground drum

urging me to wrap you
in a thousand down comforters,
feather you away from the rockslides
known to break loose
on this side of the mountain.

Angel Who Must Be Reminded

When she forgets she is an angel,
she sleeps and eats and drinks too much,
slinks off to bed or off to
white out of Chardonnay...
to erase her life's mistakes,
whatever those may be.
Does she see me as one of them?

Why doesn't she remember
she has two loving sons,
an ex-husband who is a true friend,
a lover who adores her,
goddess children who hold her dear
from her years of communal living?

Does she forget her decades-long friendship
with Yemi from Nigeria, once her *au pair*,
her ongoing art heartedness with her
best friend from high school, Kandy;
her former cooperative living pals in Wales
who raised goats with her in a backyard in London;
the slew of communal *compadres*
she lived with in the '70s in the Haight
who still love to laugh at dear Pep's act-it-out antics;
her two sisters and three brothers; or her mother
she cares for during long visits to New Jersey?

Does she not remember how her friends praise
the tasty meals she prepares for them?
Can she not touch, line up the weekly
works of art she creates and gifts to others?

Why doesn't she see her own grace,
recall her service
in the Peace Corps in The Gambia
helping set up a batik collective, still there today,
or appreciate her week-day number crunching for
homeless and battered women and children.

All these people form a Greek chorus,
chant "angel, angel" into her ear
so she will not forget who she is.

35th Anniversary (Oscar Prediction 2004)

The hearts of small children are delicate organs. A cruel beginning in this world can twist them into curious shapes.
                 —Carson McCullers, *The Ballad of the Sad Café*

Charlize Theron put on thirty pounds,
gained a badass attitude
to portray a woman who turned
a gun barrel from her own head
to the chest of a rapist,
a woman who exploded
into killing spree.

Charlize Theron watched her mother
shoot her abusing stepfather dead
when she was fifteen.

You inherited a murderous rage
passed from your mother's hands
through a thick rope wound tightly
around your little girl neck.
You spit anger through your fists
into your lover Ann's face.

Blood and bruise cooled you.
Stunned at what slept beneath your skin,
you moved out; fear crept in.

Your molten rage, doused in cold regret,
hardened into bullet metal.
In your newly-rented,
empty apartment on Winter street
you shoved that bullet
into a small-chambered gun,
used it to quell a riot in your brain.

Who's going to pay
to clean these stains from my carpet?!
the landlady screamed.

What will Charlize Theron say
when she takes the Oscar into her hands?

40th Anniversary (Time Pieces)

(2009)
July / she will fly / and give no warning to her flight.
— Paul Simon, "April Come She Will"

1.

The wall clock in the kitchen
leaks time like a faucet;
seconds drip aloud as its battery dies;
hands fold toward three-twenty,
not the arms-wide reality of five,
as if a hundred minutes have puddled
somewhere on the yellow tile floor.

2.

In the living room, a square, crystal clock
sits inside a brass rim, makes no sound;
its second hand hops from dot to dot
without calling attention to itself.
If it spoke, it would have a British accent;
but it is silent, this only clock in the house
that tells the truth.

3.

The clock radio on the side of the bed
keeps the night in a vigil of green,
miniature lanterns lighting the shore
as I lift anchor toward dreams;
come morning, these emerald digits
alarm me, blinking how little time I have
before the day is no longer my own.

4.

Gold dashes for numbers, the Seiko on my arm
is a gift; I wear the face on the inside of my wrist,
the way you did that sixth summer of our friendship,
the summer we crushed taboo with flesh;
I wear it the way you always wore yours
forty years ago, before you took the pills,
before you used the gun, before
you stopped my clocks for so many years to come.

Limerance *

One moment your life is a stone in you,
and the next, a star.
  —Ranier Maria Rilke

I come to you in ghostspell,
you wrap me in velvet,
by flicker of candlelight,
urge me back into this world.

Fusion, fire, starlight
that may well not survive,
but we chance it,
telling ourselves
that dying stars
are aquifers.

If we are not exploding supernova
and hold as steady sun,
may we wake from this celestial dream
and dream here on solid earth:
of covering chemistry of *amor*
with paraffin of *quan yin*,**
creating a treasure box of *locos focos****
we can strike anytime, anywhere.

*   in-love-ness
**   the goddess of compassion
*** the original name for matches (crazy lights)

World Cup

You beat the boys in all the races.
Best x-chrome athlete in school, you
couldn't be on a soccer team
because you were a girl.

You are up before dawn
every morning now
waiting for a kickoff, waiting
for fading light rays from
South Korea and Japan,
as your sun explodes
just above curve of horizon.

I am six thousand miles away,
in California,
waiting between
the teams and you.

Senegal one-nils France,
its old colonizer;
USA wins three-nil
against super-players of Portugal—
big upset.

We walked into each other's arms
just before the cup began last time,
four years back;
we have been in marathon since,
racing to snap the ribbon…
only a month to go.

Jersey girl, you are common-law European now—
after a quarter of a century across the pond,
married, raising two sons,
but you are becoming a single woman,
returning to America, to me.

I don't know anything about this game
you're daring me to play.
One moment I am a deer in headlights,
frozen, as you drive toward me, next
I am a filled vessel,
waiting for you to spill me.

Home Alone

Coming home
to your habit,
of leaving
the tops unscrewed
on the olive oil
and the cinnamon,
I pine for you.

Apart for twenty-one days—
a walk in the park,
a paddle on the lake—
easy time, considering
how far we have come
holding our breath
under water of time.

Best of both worlds:
you alive beside me as lusty-lucky love,
you inspiring me from beyond horizon.

I am too busy to wash the dishes tonight;
I leave them in the sink till morning
to sit, breathe, smile, think about
loving you.

G.R.I.T.S. ... Girls Raised in the South

for my cousin Trudy

My *yes sir, no ma'am* Melanie longed to be
your *sneak out the bedroom window*
after Granny goes to sleep Scarlett.
As I read *Guideposts* to the old couple across the street,
you go out with a boy in a turquoise Chevy to the lock and dam
and don't come home until just before midnight.
In my Girl Scout green or peppermint pink striped uniforms
I watch you slither into tight red skirts and twist to Chuck Berry.

Nearly half a century later you are Melanie
lifting your grandchildren, though it's bad for your back,
reminding those around you, who never have, not to drink or smoke.
You babysit with your grown kid's kids, don't see movies yourself,
and drive a mile up the road to tuck our 89-year-old Aunt Josephine
into her bed at The Home, seven nights a week.

After years living far away, I have become
what you must only imagine as Scarlett,
and you probably think some Rhett's *frankly, my dear*
has made me the way I am.
No, I have always loved women,
and now I am just shimmying my way
across the dance floor toward the gates of hell,
in that green velvet dress pieced together
from those front window drapes I finally ripped down.

Love's Arc

It begins as horses nuzzling against each other's necks,
shy, lathered in affection, explodes into
puppies, grass exclamation marks flying behind them,
galloping and re-galloping the lawn,
rushing each other over and over, nipping,
falling, rolling.

It is eagles soaring
to a mountaintop aerie in the fiery dawn,
then banyan tree monkeys
grooming each other in the noonday sun,
shifting into moss-greened oaks
mottled in gold light
of summer's long, tawny evenings.

It is sparkle of diamond evolving
into lucent obsidian.

Love melts into monks floating
in flowing, brown robes
over paths along the forest floor,
snaking through the dark
holding thimblefuls of trembling light
that transform, rise again to heights,

as silver aspen leaves caressing one another
in an ever-cooling breeze, shimmering,
rolling, falling, flying, each alone,
toward the vast, snow-swollen world
beyond the roaring hearth of this one.

Magenta Orchids

When we walked hand in hand along cobblestones in Cambridge,
kissing in devilish defiance inside the oldest chapel in England,
I couldn't see it.

Hiking over rain-slicked moors in Wales,
crossing Hampstead Heath in our winter coats,
your mittened hand inside my gloved one
as we reached the closed door of Keat's home,
I never gave it a thought.

When we sat by the picture window at Harvey's on Halloween,
watching 18th & Castro fill with witches and ghosts
and drag queens sporting Madonna masks,
as we basked in the ordinariness of same-sex couples
laughing down the street arm in arm,
I did not listen for clues; I did not want to know.

As we drank Autumn beer in the only women's bar in Amsterdam—
Vivalavie— sketched and wrote in the city's marijuana coffee houses,
as you warmed my face with your hot flash hands,
and we went from van Gogh's stars
to the real ones twinkling outside in the canals,
I imagined the road stretching on forever.

When we came and went across continents to meet—
my body pressing into yours against a wall as snow fell on Brussels,
as our lips met in the dark while the moon
eclipsed above us in Mendocino—
I felt invincible.

Tonight, as I wait here for you, these memories
press against my window panes,
scratching to come in from the cold.

You are on the other side of the world now,
struggling to leave your husband and your old life,
to return for good. All the fears I never allowed
now howl like wolves just beyond the door.
I hear our thread snapping.
I stare at the magenta orchids you left for my birthday…
crazed and certain they have outlasted us.

I find this poem in a drawer
on our fifteenth anniversary.

Simple Pleasures

is the name of the San Francisco cafe where we sit close—
two women, men all around us reading newspapers,
as a group sets up instruments, readying to play.

You sketch, I scribble. You full tilt image across open pad,
as I fiddle random words on a lined page, searching
for music. The heater eats chill gusts of wind
each time the door opens, and down the street
a silver sun slips toward the sparkling, gray Pacific.

We know we don't have to take our union too far east to brush
the serrated edges of the hate; it's a short drive to *Cal-abama*.
After our first hand-in-hand walk, just over the nearby mountains,
quick apparition of punks with baseball bats rushing from the trees.

This late Sunday afternoon, we're packed in soft batting;
tender weave of drum, piano, sax, and cotton
of this city's low clouds hold, pad us;
we feel fragile, want to be coddled now.

We are women waking from social comas, sharing a sweet
and a dark roast, holding hands in this St. Francis town jazz joint,
taking back what we missed starting out in this world.

As the live musicians tap our Beat roots, we rise,
make our way home in the fog's mist. Outside
we walk arm in arm, stop beneath a lamp post,
kiss on the street.

VI

Witness

All a poet can do is warn.
—Wilfred Owen

There have been great societies that did not use the wheel,
but there have been no societies that did not tell stories.
—Ursula K. Le Guin

Jail Time

The sky begins at your feet.
　—Hopi Chant

I spent four hours and twenty minutes in a holding cell
with Native American women of Flagstaff,
women who needed health care
for their alcohol addiction,
not iron bars holding them apart
from sun and moon and hope and love.

Did these women trickle down through history
from the waterless mountains
rising in the distance outside that jail?
Were the nine-hundred-year-old spirits
of the Sinagua pueblo ruins there with us, in DNA?

The day before, students at Northern Arizona University
invited me, and the two young black men
I was hitchhiking with in '72,
to stay the night in their dorm.
There was so much to talk about then:
Watergate was breaking,
the Equal Rights Amendment
had passed the Senate,
and we all knew boys lost in the war.
The next morning police officers,
that the housemother had called,
arrested us for vagrancy.

After those four hours and twenty minutes in that jail,
I never saw those young men I was hitchhiking with again.
Two deputies drove my twenty-six-year-old
white woman persona outside the city limits
telling me, with stern auras: *hitchhiking is illegal.*

I thumbed my way the hell out of there
as soon as their patrol car drove off,
but those Native American women's
sorrowful faces came with me.

Indians and Dogs Not Allowed.
Navajo John Redhouse remembers
this sign on a restaurant in his town
when he was a child. He recalls
the first man he saw stumbling,
under the effects of alcohol,
man whose family lost their land
to a coal company.

Today, young Star Not Afraid plays his guitar,
gets his picture on the front page
of the *Navajo-Hopi Observer.*
"There is no money for a music teacher,
so I decided to teach us," Not Afraid says.
His new music club at Hopi High School
will host musicians from around the world—
The One Song Project for peace.
Hopi means *peaceful people.*

Praise the resilient elders, the John Redhouses,
praise the new generation of Star Not Afraids.
Praise Ada Deer for saving the Menominee Tribe
from extinction by the Federal government,
for becoming the first woman to run
the Bureau of Indian Affairs;
Praise Cree, Oscar-winning musician, Buffy Sainte-Marie;
praise National Book Award Winners
Spokane/Coeur d'Alene humorist, Sherman Alexie
and Louise Erdrich, Ojibway;
praise crazy brave poet/musician
Joy Harjo, Muscogee Creek.

Praise those tribe members fighting
the cruel iron-bar-apartheid.
Praise the Native Americans painting
their proud heritage beyond cave walls,
across a blue canvas of open, equal sky,
sun and hope kissing them awake each morning
into the arms of art as wildfire
burning the difficult down to its touchable essence.

Each night, may moon and love
ease those once-jailed women and all their spirit kin,
into the sweet, untroubled sleep of proud
indigenous warriors of the twenty-first century.

Bijou* of New Orleans

for Ruby Bridges on her 60th Birthday, September 8, 2014

At six she walks past fear's sibling, hate,
her shoulders high, as if there might be
something invisible lifting them.
In her white dress
with matching bow, shoes, socks,
radiant against her chocolate skin,
she beams self-possession beyond her age.

Every day of the school year
that commences in 1960,
dress-suited federal marshals,
with yellow arm bands,
escort her to a New Orleans school
where all the other parents
have withdrawn their children,
where she is now the lone student.

They tell her not to look at anyone
in the crowd around her jeering,
and they lead her past a white wall
splattered with hurled tomatoes.

With a first grader's guileless determination,
she walks America past that white wall
into a penetrating look at the slur scrawled
next to her fresh-faced innocence.

Cockroaches and mice come
to feast on her abandoned lunches,
until her Boston teacher, Mrs. Barbara Henry,
eats with her every day after this discovery,
this hint of a silent, deeper disturbance,
sleeping in the basement of her courage.

They learn together, care for one another all that year,
even as mobs outside their school's walls
shout obscenities at them.
They travel from separate worlds, unite to form
the unbreakable bond that comes from facing danger
on a battlefield in comradeship with a fellow human.
These two black and white facets of reality's diamond
cut through the steel bars of an imprisoning culture.

This child is immortalized with startling tenderness
in Norman Rockwell's painting
that President Obama hangs on a wall
inside the West Wing of The White House.
"The Problem We All Live With" Rockwell called it
when he offered it as the cover of a 1963 *Look* magazine.

It is fifty years later
when the first African American President
greets this woman who, as a child
entering her seventh year of life,
helped cut away briars of hate,
clear the trail he took to the Oval Office.

The mythology of heaven is festooned
with gold streets and shiny pearl-white gates,
while here on blue-green earth we're blessed
with incandescent, arc-like visions
of tiny, sturdy Ruby Bridges.

*something small, delicate, and exquisitely wrought

Stone Mountain

Let freedom ring from Stone Mountain of Georgia.
      —Rev. Martin Luther King, Jr., August 28, 1963

Summers my younger brother and I
climb this gargantuan, magical, bald head,
solid scoop of rock rising all by itself
from the flat Atlanta outland,
our child-sized legs struggling up
the goliath's green, scruffy sideburns
littered with dandruff of boulders and pebbles.
Uncle accomplices help us break the rules,
carve our names into its brow.

Perhaps my dimple-cheeked brother and I walked
inside the invisible footprints of Imperial Wizards
who cast a spell on the mountain
Thanksgiving night 1915, tromping over
its wild beauty, its honeysuckle vines
and pine needles, its wintering blackberry briars.
Perhaps there were still some ghostly wisps along our path
of those goblin men who mobbed to the top
lighting a fire beneath a witches' cauldron of hatred.

Its artifacts date back ten thousand years,
soapstone bowls and dish shards
from long before the Creek and Cherokee,
before the Spanish found the mountain in 1597:
very high, shining when the sun set like a fire.

President Washington warred with its Creek.
Their land was ripped from them, handed
to the State of Georgia. *Build a fire under them.*
When it gets hot enough, they'll go
said President Andrew Jackson.
Concentration camps, then trails of tears and death.

General Sherman's troops camped nearby,
as they burned through, freeing African slaves.
But on that November night, 1915,
a gang of murderers
lights a cross on the mountaintop,
men who had lynched
an innocent Leo Frank in Atlanta,
re-kindling the Civil War century's
Ku Klux Klan.
Writing history with lightning…
Southern-born President Woodrow Wilson
exclaims that same year,
championing the malignant message
of D.W. Griffith's *Birth of a Nation*,
first movie ever screened at the White House.

When my brother and I are teens,
we watch sculptors dynamite to finish carving
a Confederate monument begun in 1916,
shrine to the fight to preserve slavery:

Stonewall Jackson
    Robert E. Lee
        Jefferson Davis

in a never-ending ride together,
on horseback, across the gentle giant's face,
hooves and haunches disappearing
into a solid, gray cloud of rock.

At the end of each childhood climb,
we welcome the giant's cool green beard of trees,
never realizing that this marvel of nature,
this eons-old, sacred tribal mountain
is suffering an evil curse,
like those in the darkest of fairy tales;

or, that the hex would be lifted
by the spell-breaking words
of an African American preacher
re-consecrating the holy giant's
beloved stone temples.

Zora

She never made a steady living from her novels
or her anthropology— collections of
cullud folks big old lies.
She died broke, living in a county home,
only fifty-nine.

She took us to jook joints in Florida in the '30s,
sat us down on Joe Clark's friendly porch
in *Mules and Men*, told us slave tales
she gathered interviewing.
Slaves and mules— bought, sold, worked too hard.
The black woman is the mule of the world she said.

Queen of the Harlem Renaissance,
she wrote plays with Langston Hughes,
used people from her life to breathe life
into the characters she gave birth to on the page.

Her Janie in *Their Eyes Were Watching God*
is strong when she must shoot the rabid man she loves.
None like her in the '30s— black heroine who,
in spite of all adversity, thrives.

In Zora's breakthrough story of 1925,
young Isie sparkles against the darkness
of self-pity, shines, momentarily blinds
the evil eye of racial supremacy.
A white woman speaks the last sentence
in her "Drenched in Light," says
I want a little of her sunshine. I need it.

The future listens, however the present may shut its ears, *
one of her contemporaries wrote. She cried out,

guiding voice through the Jim Crow fog of her time:
black is beautiful! long before Black Pride
or Black Lives Matter.

Zora lies buried in a segregated cemetery
in Fort Pierce, Florida,
and when Alice Walker went to find her,
she was simply *somewhere*
in a field of waist-high weeds.

In 1973, Alice placed a granite marker there:

> *Zora Neale Hurston*
> *"Genius of the South"*
> *1901–1960*

*Alain LeRoy Locke, *The New Negro*, 1925

Mario Savio Twenty Years On

There is a time when the operation of the machine becomes so odious, makes you so sick at heart, that you can't take part, you can't even passively take part; and you've got to put your bodies upon the gears and upon the wheels, upon the levers, upon all the apparatus and you've got to make it stop.
  —Mario Savio, Sproul Plaza, University of California at Berkeley,
    December 2, 1964

Mario Savio has a fever of 106,
ice packs all along the side of his chest
and his arms and legs,
the first time that I see him.

After his drenched sheets dry,
this curly-haired wordsmith with enkindling eyes
presses through pine needles, honeysuckle vines
of his memory, to revisit a magnolia-plush state,
land named by the Anishinabe
for its great river—*mici zibi.*

In 1964 (the 146th year of this state),
Mario Savio asks a black man—
Mandinka, Ashanti, Bakongo, Dogon?—
asks this man, whose father, grandfather never voted,
if he thinks his children ever will.

For the first time
in his long, downtrodden life
avoiding the eyes of petty tyrants,
this man decides to lift his head,
walks through heat-melted air wavering
just above the town's paved road,
dripping sweat by journey's end.

I see him brushing red dust from his overalls,
taking his torn hat into both hands,
wiping his boots on the porch, stepping in.
Inside the sheriff's office, he whispers
to the sheriff's wife:
I want to redish, ma'm.

The woman pickpockets his dignity—
What's that you say, boy? What's redish?
What are you talking about, boy?
We don't got no redish around here—
taunts him from her perch of power.
Mario tells this story as if it is happening now,
feels the iron chains of helplessness
clapped on him by a law demanding his silence.

He speaks in a soft, whispery voice himself,
as if he does not want to disturb, as if he is in awe,
of the brave man standing his ground
while a verbal whip of abasement rains down.

As he spills more sad epiphanies of Freedom Summer
twenty years before, more troubled in these moments
than in all the difficult weeks of his hospital ordeal,
the alarm on the IV bleeds into his story.
I turn to the machine, then back to the crook of his arm—
he is healing and will go on to master physics,
teach philosophy and mathematics in Sonoma,

this thoughtful, almost bashful man
whose words struck a global lightning bolt
on the steps of Berkeley's Sproul Hall,
shy spearhead of the Free Speech Movement,
who removed his shoes to do no harm
to the police car he climbed,
standing on its roof in sock feet
to frenzy a crowd of three thousand.

But today, he is melancholy and far away, lost in the landscape
of cotton fields and blackberry briars, *mici zibi* inside him rising,
as the great, great, great grandchild of a kidnapped African slave
makes a move, lights a fire, signals down the decades
in Mario Savio's Abraham Lincoln eyes.

Sunday in the Temple of Democracy

The public library has always been a powerful force against inequality.
—Ian Frazier, *The New Yorker*, June 2, 2014

Saturday we see *12 Years a Slave*,
movie made from a memoir
of a citizen of New York
kidnapped into the miasma
of one race subjugating another.
After the lights are up
and the theater is emptying,
we struggle like swimmers in trouble
to come up to this century's air.
After we rise from this rendering
of an American Holocaust,
we walk out into the evening light
that is just leaving us.

Sunday, back at work, I help
a stooped African American grandmother
who struggles to schedule an appointment online
for a visit with her grandson in prison.
She frets in a lather of self-effacement
over her troubles with usernames and passwords.
She apologizes for taking up
too much of my librarian time.

Swimming in yesterday's waters,
I touch her arm, catch her eye.
I watch her shoulders loosen,
her texture go from burlap to velour,
her face lift and smile, as I tell her
You are my boss; I work for you.

Charlotte's Web

*—for my niece, Nicole, who, unlike her aunt, remains on the front lines,
nursing with profound skill and fierce empathy*

On the first night with that new nurse,
Charlotte heard her call and wake
some poor, sleep-deprived intern
to confirm she should really give
the triple dose syringe of medicine ordered.

Of course it should have killed a woman her size,
now eighty-three pounds, but the lung cancer
had metastasized to her bones— it was the weight
of her pain, not her flesh, that mattered.

Charlotte heard by the near-tears of her voice
that this one has to be broken in, handled with
velvet gloves so as not to scratch her into
uselessness. Charlotte didn't throw things at her
as she did the others— blood pressure cuffs, vases;
she hated having to write everything down that she
wanted to say. This nurse was a bleeding heart—
you could see she needed to be out of here
away from code blues, bedpans, blood.

Why couldn't Charlotte have gotten one of those
stoic perfectionists for these cough-and-fear-filled nights,
not this tenderfoot who might be shocked into sloppiness.
Christ, she was dying; she shouldn't have to worry about
some damned nurse's psyche while she wasted away.
It would block her trachea, she would suffocate—
thank God it was down to days.

Nursing Elizabeth

Little he knew, poor death-stricken boy, the heart of the stranger that hover'd near.

  —Walt Whitman in *Specimen Days* (June, 1863, as he nursed a Union
    soldier dying from a bullet–pierced lung)

She wobbles, shoving an IV pole along the hallway,
taking chocolate to the patient next door who has
swapped rooms with her. She is determined
to reward this young man for giving her his bed
with a view of the Golden Gate Bridge
and its majestic fog sculpture.
Somewhere beneath the cosmetic face
she dabs on each day, a secret part of her
reacts as if this will be her last window,
though no one has told her yet
and she has not yet told herself.

I watch her put together jig-saw fragments,
discover a picture: she has no friends,
only acquaintances.
I am there each time her doctor
tells her the chemo isn't working,
I hear the story of her missing family,
her lost World War II fiancé,
I listen to her memory of herself at three
falling from a window while watching
one of the first-ever airplanes.

I hear her spin tales of fictitious futures
when she cannot look death in the eye,
witness her rage sucked savagely
into the vacuum of her universe;
I hold her when she cries, cool her face,
feel the sun of her bony grin

when we lift her swollen body
into the relief of a warm bath.

Desperate, she lets me near her crushing world
at first, lets me soothe her; but at the end
there is nothing I can do, except
measure the morphine with precision,
deliver it on time.

Her eyes are a tincture of fire and fear
the last time I see her.
She speaks from a skeletal face
in a high, raspy, alien voice, shrieks
Get away from me!
with more energy than she owns,
and death forecloses.

First Club

They took cabs from the hospital to Dennis's home,
hoping for marijuana.
After he paid their cab drivers, they came inside,
smoked in his living room.

He brought plates of spaghetti,
baskets of garlic bread,
bunches of grapes and bananas,
bowls of vanilla ice cream…

after the THC quelled the queasiness,
made them hungry again
for the first time in weeks.

No one stuck wires to their skin
or examined their urine;
without a microscope
everyone could *see them eat,*
stop dying of starvation.

They would laugh, lying right there next to Death,
fall into a deep, healing sleep, get up, smoke, keep eating,
live years longer than the ones before them.

Drug War

On the first day of the New Year,
your name appears in bold print
in papers across the nation.
Associated Press blows up your words,
quotes you in a breakout box
criticizing the President.

All seventy-six pounds of you
stands upright inside the boxing ring
of this nationally publicized fight.
On the ropes, you still get off
a powerful jab at the nose of government.

Inside, your immunity is down for the count,
but the fourth antibiotic tried
finally picks off bacteria in your blood
like tin cans off a fence post at close range.

We bring you Alice B. Toklas brownies,
but you have no appetite, cannot eat them.
Only smoke keeps you from disappearing.

When We Visit Ina for the Last Time

When we visit Ina for the last time,
she looks forward to us,
as a child looks forward
to Christmas or Hanukkah.
She's out of bed, out of pajamas,
short bristly-gray hair combed
an hour before we ring the bell,
unlike yesterday when
she couldn't get out of bed.

We ride the elevator to her third floor
and when she opens to us I can see
the loneliness of death has set in.
Food isn't working; she's stopped writing;
she doesn't feel all that well.
She keeps her wraith under the covers now.
We are a short, sweet break
from the bleakness of it all.

She thanks us for not saying the word *cancer*
out loud, puts half an Alice B. Toklas ginger snap
into her frail body, and one hour later
makes us smoke to be with her.
Surprised by appetite, she chows down
the Chinese food we've brought, grins, amazed.

Our words dance together,
then Ina's high takes over,
silences her sharp, now fragile, mind
with constant short term memory loss
that triggers runaway laughter—
she convulses, unable to speak.

Her lifespark lights the room—
wildfire—
as tears run down her cheeks
and all our bellies hurt;
salty mix of joy and grief
pours from her poetry place.
Teeth, gums, more teeth— she cannot stop laughing.
Some part of her becomes a graceful bird, a heron,
rising toward heaven on those great winds
she has already surrendered to.

City College Poets

for June

... the darkness around us is deep.
—William Stafford

It was her eyes that first made me think
she might be standing in quicksand up to her knees.
They were animal-beaten-by-owner eyes
that never looked up from the page
as she read to us in class
from her spun silk word-threads.

We cooperated to enter our poems
in an *American Pen Women* contest,
mentored by our professor,
partner of the late and treasured poet,
William Dickey.

We walked up Mt. Parnassus in San Francisco
to hear Robert Hass, our then-U.S. Poet Laureate.
She laughed, pleased she was making a friend,
glistening with a shy wit that surprised me.
Afterward, when we went for a snack,
she had no cash. Embarrassed,
she accepted only coffee from me.

With sun splashed affect she spoke of
her boyfriend having hit her as if it were long ago.
Some hint of how she spoke it—
the too bright coloring of her words perhaps—
made me want to eat chocolate,
bite my nails, or drink a beer.

The next week she phoned to say
she wouldn't make class, voice high-pitched
and tinged with *something's wrong*.

Though we'd only shared poems
and met just twice outside of that,
though she talked about
her angry boyfriend in past tense,
a sentry voice inside me whispered
invite her to your guest room,
while a deeper, fearful me thought:
he might find her here.
This all not quite conscious,
not falling on me like rain,
more like a fine mist
that I could pretend
was not really there
dampening things.

My address book holds her name,
and I held a wisp of her smoky spirit for a moment—
fragile poet losing her struggle with a violent lover.

A week after her death, I learn
I've won the prize in the contest we entered—
for a poem called "Lament."

Seeing Stars: Haight Holiday, 2007

for Daniel, David, Dennis, & Gene

The homeless are well fed in the city of St. Francis
on this Christmas Day: the streets are deserted
as if a plague or hurricane might be on the way.

A cold, sunlit silence has fallen on the streets,
the hum of humanity is missing,
the shops are closed, there are no runaways,
no skateboarders.

From the jungles of Vietnam
a grizzled survivor emerges,
steps through the bushes of the park
beside the streetcar tracks,
asks for a quarter or a smoke.

Catty-corner from him
a black, Iraq-aged man appears,
sweating vodka, singing loud and off-
reason, flailing his arms skyward,
in a private triumph,
in front of a closed yuppie wine bar
where a purple and red woven star
hangs in its picture window.

A car breaks the roadway silence,
turns a corner at Ashbury and Waller,
its bumper sticker commenting:
Will Rogers Never Met George Bush.

The day wears its erratic patterns
as the sun retreats to the Pacific horizon.
An eight-foot tall camellia bush

on Stanyan Street, clothed in yesterday's
rain-soaked flowers and buds,
blinks on a string of multi-colored lights
hung on its branches like strands of pearls.

Outside the Hamilton Shelter, two friends
stand together on the sidewalk
digesting a free, holiday meal,
talking in low tones
about a vet buddy's mind field
and the silver star that hangs over it.
The moon's once Cheshire cat grin rises,
transformed now to round-faced Buddha,
charcoal tattoo streak veined
along one glowing, yellow-gold cheek.
The wind blasts away high clouds
and the first bright star of this holiday evening
flares, gleams, takes command
of a small, dark sector of sky above them.

The Leaves of the Linden Tree*

One death is a tragedy; one million is a statistic.
—Joseph Stalin

Our heads buzzed.
Our eyes were too dry to blink.

At night carts rolled
through the streets
collecting bodies.

A black flag flying
over a village
meant everyone
who had lived there
was dead.

Stalin stole their farms
ordering the victims
to work for him.
Those who refused
were kulaks;
kulaks were vermin.

In the frozen winter of 1932,
I was nearly gone
when my mother found
four hedgehogs
in a pile of hay
she had gathered as fuel.
She boiled them in a pot.
I ate and grew stronger.

The words *hunger* and *famine*
were banned
in this record year
of grain export
from these Ukrainian fields.

I was seven
when I watched my mother
wrest a knife from my father's hands
stopping him from cutting his own throat.

In this year, Amelia Earhart
flies across the Atlantic,
Gandhi fasts on behalf
of the Untouchables,
Hitler edges closer to power,
and *Brave New World* is published.
The Nobel Committee decides
not to award a Peace Prize.

Families were shoved into rail cars
headed for gulags in Siberia.
They threw our children off the trains
into white mounds of snow.

All food belonged to the State.
He hid a small stalk of wheat
under his coat;
they cut off his hand.
By decree, they confiscated
potatoes, carrots, livestock.

We saw a woman protest
that her daughter
was still moving her arms and legs
as she lay on the side of the road.

The workers still tossed her
on top of the cart piled with bodies.
'She will be gone as soon as we leave.
We may as well take her with us now.'

No one was allowed in or out,
but smuggled letters made it
to the American Secretary of State.
They called us white moths
as they watched us starve.
Parents kept their children
at home for safety.
We killed dying children
and ate them.
Stalin's wife, Nadya,
fired a bullet into her heart.

In the spring of 1933,
as the snow began to melt
and the world began to green,
they stumbled from their homes
to the forests,
after up to ten million of them were gone.

The leaves of the linden tree
tasted best of all.

*Poem written November 23, 2013, following an 80th Anniversary Commemorative ceremony in San Francisco honoring the victims of the Ukrainian Holodomor (murder by starvation), 1932-1933, the largest genocide recorded in all of human history. The words in italics are exact or very close approximations of the testimony heard this day from survivors.

The Dancers

(an etching by Camilla Hall, circa 1971)

I.

She breathes in Matisse's *Dance,*
exhales it as something else—
breasts, butts, bellies sway
in weightless exuberance,
feet tap hallelujahs in mid-air;
arms are one long ribbon rippling
through the bodies of four women:
art of a Midwest minister's daughter
who has just come out.

We gather every week through the summer of '72—
me, Camilla, her scowling lover, Mizmoon,
in a lush, green Berkeley backyard that I drive to in a truck
from my boyfriend's house in rustic Forest Knolls,
where I've dropped mescaline and suddenly know
I don't belong with him anymore.
We become a ring of seven,
women circling against a disease tag
psychiatrists are still two years from giving up.

Jan invites me to move to San Francisco,
into her lesbian sandwich, a middle floor
between two flats of half-baked gay men
living proud and outrageous in smoke-filled rooms,
while Jan's friend, Dick, fox living with the hens,
gooses us as we wash our dishes, grabs our breasts
as we lift a can of tuna from a top shelf.

Breezy, blond Camilla, whose art is her day job,
visits us from time to time,

rumbling to our house in her yellow VW Bug.
We welcome her champagne essence, bubbling the air around us;
through wire-framed glasses her eyes become cartoon slits,
as if she is taking aim at us with her cheer.
She climbs our stairs one afternoon,
in aqua socks and cut-off overalls, holding back tears,
invites me to share a peyote trip. Her mirthless lover
has just dropped her.

I buy Camilla's etching, my first art purchase ever,
hang its crimson frame against my new white wall
at this this loosey goosey community on Arguello Street,
near Golden Gate Park.

II.

Three years later,
long after our women's group has stopped gathering—
and I've moved from Jan's home to escape Dick's gropes—
I see Camilla through the window of my TV set.
She and Mizmoon have kidnapped Patty Hearst.
Two men in their Symbionese Liberation cult
have shot Marcus Foster to death,
the first black to head the Oakland schools.

I study photos of Camilla's face on the nightly news for months,
thinking there is some, yet unexplained, mistake,
until one cool, fog-filled afternoon in San Francisco,
I fall through the cathode ray tube,
tumble into the stifling heat of Los Angeles in May,
beside Camilla— and Mizmoon— again,
this time crawling on the floor, beneath whiz of bullets
and the kiss of their wind, sweating
as fire dances toward our feet.

III.

Tonight, decades later, I watch a documentary about the SLA,
learn something new after thirty-five years— it was Mizmoon
who murdered Marcus Foster, not the men,
Mizmoon who fired the shot that began it.

I watch the police raid their safe house again
on a television set that sits below Camilla's etching,
still inside its blood-red frame—
dancers in cryogenic joy, cool star
above mad, ravenous flames consuming all.

Drawing Joseph Out About Stonewall

To burn with desire and keep quiet about it is the greatest punishment we can bring on ourselves.
　　—Federico Garcia Lorca, *Blood Wedding*

Judy Garland had just slipped over the rainbow a week before,
pressing a gray fog of melancholy into the corners of their lives
as they listened to her disembodied voice—
siren songs of Saharan loneliness, rhapsodies of mad, lush love.
Her father was gay, and two of her five husbands;
her Dorothy lived in a black and white world, like theirs,
before dreaming it into glorious Technicolor.

On this sultry New York City night in June,
shy, asthmatic Joseph trembled on the train,
making his way, for the first time,
to an underground gathering place in the Village,
telling his old world Italian parents
he was staying the night at a classmate's home.
At nineteen, the icy winter of his adolescence
was thawing into spring.

As he entered the bar, Joseph stood agog against a wall,
watching the drag queens teeter on heels,
bat the butterfly wings of their lashes,
flip their boas as they walked past him.
He stood near the lesbians, in jackets and ties,
and nearly passed out, when a manful man,
wearing a suit and a movie star smile,
asked him to dance.

It was the happiest moment of my life until then, he recalled:
I can still hear Diana Ross and the Supremes
throbbing "Love Child" as he touched my hand.
I couldn't look at him for a moment—

I thought I might cry from joy, right there on the dance floor.
When I did look up, I wanted to kiss his sculpted face,
but this Greek god, electrifying my hand in his,
snapped an iron cuff on my wrist.

The paddy wagons were delayed, but the lit fuse
burning so close to my tinderbox core, was unstoppable by then.
As the cops herded us out to the front of the Stonewall Inn,
and a crowd gathered to jeer at them, drunk with fear of exposure,
still wanting to kiss that man, I heaved a gray, steel trash bin
into the heart of a plate glass window.

Pink Rain

Dateline: Medford, Oregon, December 6, 1999

No one knows yet where they are
when night rolls in as black fog.

The police have been notified;
it is 48 hours since they were last seen.

Those close fear the worst, as they search
for two lovers outspoken about tolerance.

As the winter solstice nears, newspapers
scream countrywide troglodyte violence.

> *I'm going to kill me a Chinaman*
> from a white who stabs an Asian
> outside a California supermarket.
>
> *We're going to loot and burn the Jews*
> incites a black to torch a store in Harlem,
> char eight. Suicide arsonist.
>
> U.S. Army skinheads, with Nazi flag and
> *Natural Born Killers* tape, gun down
> random black couple in North Carolina.

A three-year-old watches her mother cry,
tugs at her arm, asks *Where's Grandma?*

She cannot name, but inhales the fear
for Grandma Roxanne, Baba Michelle.

She's someone's grandma for God's sake.
Isn't that sick? I don't care for lesbians
the killer later says, expressing no regret.

With dawn's gray shards and wet storminess,
they will be discovered in their cold, steel-canopied bed.

Tonight, in a parking lot across town, pink rain
trickles from the bottom seam of their truck's tailgate.

This season of peace on earth, goodwill
brings diversity of hatred.

Family, friends, strangers will grieve, gather, mourn, survive;
they will live
lives devoted to healing from this fabric-ripping storm
inside their own private Idaho of the human condition.

Postcard from the Castro

*Two days after I was elected I got a phone call and the voice was quite young.
It was from Altoona, Pennsylvania. And the person said 'Thanks.'... If a bullet
should enter my brain, let that bullet destroy every closet door.... You've gotta'
give them hope.*
    —Harvey Milk

Harvey Milk is smiling out a window in the Castro again,
in a new portrait on the side of his old building—
half-circle smile, head bowed,
looking out through a sliver of sun
onto the sidewalk of his old neighborhood.

He seems to know something we don't.
Or is his smile just the start of a happy laugh
remembering this gay Mecca is named Eureka Valley?
Maybe he's simply admiring the beautiful boys
holding hands with such nonchalance
as they sashay past him heading toward
Does Your Mother Know on 18th.
He has the radiance of someone who sees through hate,
from this window on a wall, rainbow flag across his chest,
rainbows fluttering from lamp posts at every corner.

The van Gogh golds and blues of the mural
hang like a lodestar above his once open-to-all refuge,
his Castro Camera store, his first openly gay supervisor's
campaign office, this hippie community center
where I once sat in his old dentist's chair installed
like a work of beat art in the middle of his shop floor.
I knew him when I did not know who I was.

Looking back on the long journey from then to now:
his holy, disarming comedy silenced
by a deadly-serious, fear–spawned loathing...

yet out of that sudden, bloody silence, a roar—
from Altoona, Pennsylvania, San Antonio, Des Moines.

I have come here on a pilgrimage from the Haight:
I'm alive, I'm in love, I'm in hope, I'm out.
His image shines like a moon over Castro Street again,
but I cannot meet the gaze of his hidden, earthcast eyes.

If I could, I would say:
Thanks, Harvey.
Having a wonderful time.
Wish you were here.

41st Anniversary (Measured Healing)
(2010)

Perhaps the virus of slavery leapt from a colony of ants
on the edge of the Mesopotamian desert
sickening infant humankind in 3000 B.C.,
as it rolled away from hunt and gather,
crawling toward greater clusters of cooperation.
It ravaged Babylon, Egypt, Greece, West Africa, Baghdad,
poisoned the Portuguese, British, Dutch,
hit the Caribbean, the Americas,
fevered through humanity, erupting in blisters of horror and war.

Your mother tried to hang you,
your foster mother beat you with a rubber hose.

Lashed skin is vulnerable to the microbe of despair
that enters, breaches heart muscle, leaves soul syphilitic,
open sores passing contagion on and on,
by casual contact or through birth canals, to bystanders
or children of children of children beyond the whip
who do not know they are touched by it.

Slides project against my mind's wall,
me, unaware, at a wedding shower,
you drugged, bloody, already dead.

Haitian rebels and pacifist Brits,
on opposite sides of the globe in the 1800s,
forced a Pasteur epiphany, as humans began
to understand bondage as pathogen of illness.
In Jamaica they buried the chains, but the bacillus
still thrives in the topsoil of the present.

When someone confides an abused childhood,
I put the storyteller on suicide watch.
Today is the 41st anniversary of your violent break
from the heavy chains of trauma.

The healing will be slow, measured best
in one hundred year increments.

Winter of Love

(Valentine's Day San Francisco 2004)

At the front entrance of City Hall, exultant couples
walk out through open glass doors, holding hands
and licenses that flutter in their grasp like flags.

A tiptoe rain mizzles red, gold,
pink, lavender rose petals
quilting the palatial stone steps;
multi-colored umbrellas wait outside like limos.

The crowd cheers loudly every few minutes all day long,
as pair after pair of women, pair after pair of men
walks out through the city's gray mist
into rainbow, rainbow, rainbow.

VII
Winter of Love

I shall be richer all my life for this sorrow.
—Wallace Stegner, *All the Little Live Things*

Tragedy is like strong acid—
it dissolves away all but the very gold of truth.
—D. H. Lawrence

Joy was a flame in me
Too steady to destroy;
Lithe as a bending reed
Loving the storm that sways her—
—Sara Teasdale

May the stars carry your sadness away,
May the flowers fill your heart with beauty…
—Chief Dan George

St. Frances of Augusta

I look like the devil before daylight
Aunt Frances told us after she got sick
and did not want us taking pictures.

Lawd, honey, my 'lectric lights are off for sure
(meaning sodium and potassium).
Call the doctor, I feel like forty miles of bad road she said,
wrapping herself in a silken comforter of Southern poetry,
a splash of Cotton Blossom behind her ear,
a quarter moon smile always rising above her pain.

As a child I was bewitched by this raven-haired Marilyn—
her luminous beauty swooning over Frank Sinatra,
eyes twinkling as she alto-ed "Love and Marriage"
and The Andrews Sisters' "Sisters"
into the melodies of our lives,
fingers tap dancing on piano keys,
body swaying, palm in a soft breeze.

She lived by an unspoken creed:
when the grown-ups have their troubles,
the children must have glee,
and two years after her scandalous '50s divorce,
she gathered up her daughter,
my mother, my brother, and me,
sweet-talked her red-haired boyfriend, Louis,
into driving us all three hundred miles to Daytona Beach:

salty scent and taste of sea, bubbly laughs as Atlantic waves
tumble us into sundown; warm, de-sanding showers,
attentive eyes of her Louis, and his strong, lifeguard arms.

As she aged inside a second marriage
to a spitting image of John Wayne,
she sang and played only Methodist hymns,
gave up the tunes of the "Hit Parade,"
but, *I'm madder'n a mule with a mouth full of bees,*
she might say, backlighting her Jesus-love
with flickers of divine devilishness.

Like a Rosemary Clooney hit single
twirling inside me when I was little,
her soft *Hey, Dahlin* spins and spins
on my memory's turntable.
Her voice is backyard churned ice cream
melting over warm peach pie.

I secretly snap a picture, put it up at her memorial:
our aging, angelic, bluesy, even-in-sickness-beautiful aunt,
not smiling, but looking out toward eternity with a brave quiet,
woman always tender with our fragile vase of childhood,
silver hair radiant against her purple robe.

Watchpuppy, or What It's Like to Be a Feeler

I dream that long after I'm gone, my work will go on helping people.
—Isabel Myers, Feeler, co-creator of the Myers-Briggs Type
Indicator

Inside my psyche's fence a dozing puppy's
eyelids twitch, as she chases jays
across my mind's yard in her sleep;
but if someone comes, she knows right away;

her tail starts wagging before her lids lift.
Her nose whiffs a thousand more pieces
of information than mine ever will;
she can smell a broken heart at thirty paces.

This idiot savant guards my boundaries,
sniffs out pheromones of pain and fear,
the fragrances of human insecurity,
cancer on breath, the scent of need in tears.

I've never been able to train her to bark intruders away;
her paw always scratches open the gate.

M'Aidez

She is a dry sponge of need
sealed inside a plastic wrap of insecurity.
Look-at-me-love-me thirst drives her
as she crashes over and over again
against her own polyvinyl chloride boundary.

Was it lightning strike—
an abusive, alcoholic father, or death
of a mother when she was five—
or did the desiccation and sealing
come with living her life on the sandy beaches
of her husband's and children's oceanic lives?
Did she dehydrate by damming
her own rivers of creativity,
or by syphoning away the juiciness
of her true sexual nature?

Whatever the reasons,
her *élan vital* is desert-floor-dry
behind a homemade hazmat suit
she does not know is there.

She can see praise,
but it never soaks past her shield;
and she wants more, more,
but I am not brave enough
to deliver the pin pricks
that might help soft moisture
of compassion to leak in.

If only there were a Code Purple to call,
a compassion ER, a psych ICU,
some kind of emergency soul surgery,

or an alarm to pull
bringing brawny trauma fighters
in slickers and big rubber boots,
aiming the full force of their
milk of human kindness hoses,
dissolving her stifling, strangling,
see-through prison wall,
soaking her with a liquid *quan yin*
she is driven to bathe others in.

In That Sleep of Death

For in that sleep of death what dreams may come…
— William Shakespeare, *Hamlet*

Are there dreams in the sleep of the dead;
do the perished sail on lucid rivers
of longing and memory of breath;
do they jolt with illusion of rising,
have nightmares if they died violently?

Do they run in the dark,
their legs carrying them nowhere;
are there unexpected tests and failures,
recurrent guilt that can't be shaken,
as they wear pajamas to the office,
dance naked on the freeway?

Are they late for their weddings, or lost
in majestic, primeval forests
crawling with snakes and panthers;
do they laugh about sex with Jung or Freud
while smoking Havana cigars;
do they dream of abandonment by God?

As they soar on winds in effortless flight,
do they sense
the mysterious presence of the living?

Soul's Flora

> *Your soul is a chosen landscape.*
> —Paul Verlaine

The soul selects her own softscapes—
scarlet sage, Queen Anne's lace, blue columbine—
that thrive against the hardscapes
of granite mountainsides.

In hot desert sands, *alma* decorates
with tumbleweed swept away in Santa Ana winds,
or irrigates date palm oases.
Seele's edelweiss could be crushed under jackboots,
or fly in white hot rebellion from a rocky crevasse.

On the frozen tundra of tyranny,
dusha may seed saxifrage,
kindle miles of earth
with bright magenta fire-food.
Ziel might add the beauty of orchids and tulips
to the dike holding back a flood of despair.

Bending beechwood into gondola,
anima can float above
dark, viscous canals of sorrow.

Nafsi might grow the vibrant African violet
that takes death's breath away
in a dense jungle of hatred.
Âme chooses to follow orders,
weed an imprisoned mother and child,
or feeds and waters them in defiance
through the barbed wire fence of a *V'el d'Hiv*.

Genes or happenstance may trap us in the swamps,
the dunes, the quarries, or gift us
the lagoons, savannas, forests of our lives.
But *soul* plants the nettle or the rose,
the poison ivy or the marigold.

To the Lighthouse

The alcoholic upstairs has fallen again, shit himself, broken a rib.
The doctors have him long enough to give him blood,
teach him to walk again,
while we go up and down his twenty-nine steps twice a day,
feed and pet his orphaned cat.
How many more nights of cackles, sobs,
country songs throbbing through the floor boards,
how many more times will we call 9-1-1
before he passes from his liquid heaven above us?

Born to his single mother at age fourteen,
my daughter's godson opens the gate to a private high school
with his curious mind, his basketball moves,
then slams himself behind prison walls
trying for the rich kids' jeans and shoes, apologizing,
the victims say, as he stole their phones with a toy gun—
clumsy, sad trip down the river to the new Jim Crow—
six years— then a lifetime of second tier.

A poet comrade dies,
another gay teen is bullied into suicide,
Aung San Suu Kyi is so tired…
winds of stress press us against brick walls of our daily lives,
until midday we inch into the safety of our hubcap-less Corolla,
disappear up the rocky Pacific coast.

Day stars shimmer on the surface of the sea,
on this rare warm, transparent day at the Point of Kings.
We hike past windswept Monterey cypress,
tule elk, blood-red lichen,
descend a cascade of stairs,
wrap ourselves in salty calm, honor the guardians
who lit oil lamps during crashing storms,
saving seafarers from pounding, watery death
a hundred and fifty years ago.

Strong iron rails cradle us above the precipice
as a tender wind touches our faces,
and two teenage whales, escapees
from the great Southern Migration,
spout, breach below us.

Kindred runaways, we watch them
frolic in gleaming, backlit blue-green waves,
fold our arms around each other in delight,
leaning, again and again,
out over this windiest tip
of western continental America—
a bejeweled finger of land—
hoping to sight them one more time.

As the day begins to leak away,
we take a thirty-story climb,
up from this rocky outpost,
drive back into our quotidian lives,
open our garden room door
to the glow of family and friends
surprising me for my sixty-fifth birthday.

The blazing oil lamps of their tribal faces,
glance a rhythmic light into my mind,
guide me next morning to the family
weeping together on a courtroom bench,
send me through a wispy fog after work
to my upstairs neighbor's hospital bed, yet

some slip of me remains
at the Point Reyes Lighthouse,
in that crow's nest at the edge of our world,
watching rebel whales swim
in the sea's silvery waters.

Friends for Life Denouement

Jerry went first in the early '80s, told Kathryn
he was going to commit suicide by AIDS.
He saved his Darvon in the hospital at the end,
asked Kathryn to come and help him OD.
The morning she was dressing to go to him,
the hospital called to say he was gone.

I was talking to Kathryn on the phone in the '90s,
when she started having trouble breathing.
She died in the hospital just days later,
not from the lupus she'd had from her youth,
but from the side effects of the prednisone she took
to stop her body from attacking itself.

I heard Lenora was Nancy Reagan's masseuse for a time.
What a hoot if that was true, lesbian in the Reagan White House!
I saw her photo in a book on Haight Street years ago,
a book of lesbian families.
I wrote her once, on what must have been
a defunct Facebook page, and never heard from her.

I guess this poem is really for you, Lenora,
to tattoo two treasured memories onto the page,
moments we shared after the times of MDMA
and what Carson McCullers would call
our *we of me* quartet.

One is watching you on the phone
at Suicide Prevention in Atlanta,
hotly defending a caller's right to kill himself,
building a stealth rapport with him
that may have saved his life.

The other is the week we spent together
in the French Quarter of New Orleans,
three years after that ghastly summer of '69.
It took decades for me to heal,
but your touch was oasis
on that long desert slog
out of otherworldly graveyards
back to *cafés du monde*.

Southern Dad

As he finishes the U-turn that has blocked my way,
a man in a big blue truck smiles and flashes me a V,
his fingers a surprise divining rod
unearthing a memory of an age-six me
mesmerized by my father's pantomimes
as I sit behind him on the bus he's driving.
I see him throw his arm out the window,
salute, tip his hat, blink his lights,
or nod in silent communion,
steering his wheeled blacktop ship
along rural Georgia two-lane highways
lined with blackberry bramble and pine.

His highway camaraderie made me proud
I was his daughter,
an island of pride in a curious, rising pond of shame:
a cruel teasing that sometimes boiled from him,
making it impossible to bring home friends.
Though I could not name it,
I longed for the kinder intimacy
he and these roadway strangers shared.

At that age I did not know he knew Morse Code,
or that he used it, in the Atlantic, to flicker sparks
across the icy, dark sea— *against orders*—
saving a shipful of men from death by friendly torpedo.

After the war, he wore a starched, gray
Southeastern Stages uniform,
and signaling as a civilian
may have grounded him in a way
that no one understood.

When I turn sixteen, ready to learn to drive,
he morphs into a patient, caring teacher
as I sit behind the wheel of our red VW Bug.
No mean jokes, none of the ill temper that flashed
when he gave up on my mother, dismissing her
as a student forever, after she rolled onto the curb.
As we sit on opposite sides of the stick shift,
he seems to love teaching me.

As he aged, I began weekly
long-distance archaeological digs
into the ruins of his decades-old spirit,
a delicate sifting through trivia
searching for shards of stories
that might help solve mysteries.
He talked to me while watching two TVs,
and listening to the crackling
of law enforcement officers ten-fouring each other,
as they raced to crises throughout the county.

All his life he joked that he had not seen a movie
after *Birth of a Nation*, but as I dug deeper,
I learned my father was beaten as a small boy
for trying on a white robe and hood
he found beneath his father's bed.
I mined only small bits of memoir
between that boyhood and eighty,
the year he left us wondering.

I did not know him well,
this man fired from his sixteen years of bus driving
after talking to a union rep in his own home,
man who sold Fuller Brushes and insurance
in the black ghettos on the other side
of our Civil War nostalgic town,
man who learned to repair TVs, who drove trucks

filled with dangerous canisters of hydrogen and oxygen,
losing his brakes once on his way down a mountainside in Alabama,
man who bought a gas station and hired
a black man he called his best friend to help him run it,
man who begged his wife
for his children's three hundred dollar education fund
to save him in this last of his failed entrepreneurial bets,
after which our mother drew a line in the sand, at last,
that sent them into separate lives of struggle,
just as their country began wrestling for its soul.

He was a mystery father,
this man who became a deputy sheriff after his divorce,
and could not bear to tell me in his old age
what he'd done as a man who carried a billy club and a gun.
He cried every time he tried to speak of it.

No, I did not know this stubborn, tangled man well,
but I swayed in the earthquakes of his struggles,
and honor the ghost who signaled
through seasickness on those icy waves,
risking his life to save Western civilization for me.

I think of him now each time I sign travelers on the road,
and when they hail back, they do not know
they send startling, warm and open-hearted
semaphore from my father.

Talkin' 'Bout My Bro

> *We real cool…*
> —Gwendolyn Brooks

My blues-cool brother Gene—wounded by our father,
father who did not really know how to be one—
is scorching our living room floor,
blazing through his sleek *mashed potato* moves
in his Gant shirt, pegged jeans, and Weejuns.
He and his best friend, Phil, are the only two white boys,
who go to the Bell Auditorium in Augusta, Georgia, early 1960s,
to watch James Brown, the Temptations, the Supremes,
on the *Chitlin' Circuit,*
while his older sis is home listening to Frank Sinatra
singing Johnny Mercer's *Autumn Leaves,*
trying to douse the deeper rumblings in her basement.

One evening, when his mom and sis are home
watching *Dragnet,* or *Gunsmoke,* he saunters in,
strutting across the living room
like a prince, a peacock, a young bull.
A pack of cigarettes thuds from his pocket to the floor,
but he does not stop, and his mother
does not say a word. She knows
he's drinking at age fifteen and hasn't a clue
about the best way to intervene.
It's 1964, and she's getting a divorce,
has no idea what she is in for.

He is a Renaissance Child who sketches our grandfather,
plays the guitar, aces shop class when he goes to it.
He skips school and hunts ducks
trying to make sense of the upheaval in his family world.
He remembers being left in the car when our father
would visit just a little too long
at the home of one of the women on his Fuller Brush route.

His mom and sis urge him into military school,
but this compounds his traumas.
As *The Draft* looms, he and best friend Phil join the Navy,
lied to with the promise they will serve in the same place.
By the time we are watching *Woodstock* together
in San Francisco in 1970, and I hand him his first joint,
he is on his way to the Aleutian Islands in Alaska.
Crazed by dark months of Adak in winter,
he ships out early to San Francisco...
Benicia... prelude to Vietnam.
He and his antiwar soldier buddy
drop Psilocin, an electric blue pill by Sandoz,
read Huxley's *Doors of Perception* and *Heaven and Hell.*

Sitting in the Gulf of Tonkin, he spends each day
expecting his ammo ship to be blown out of the water.
But it is when his ship is taking on
fresh ammo supplies in the Philippines,
and he sees a prostitute being beaten by police,
that he has his life-altering epiphany—
that the war and his part in it is morally repugnant.
He ships out to Guam, drops Owsley's Purple Haze—
then for five weeks we had duty two days on,
followed by three days off with Orange Sunshine.
I grew my hair long and refused to shave...
They gave up on me, and let me out early.

Now, he plays his guitar with all his soul,
fires off liberal responses to conservative bloggers
all around him in Athens, Georgia,
holding his hill, his bay, his valley, his fort.
He lives by his master carpentry skills
that come naturally to his Leo da Vinci,
and he has found the Renaissance woman love of his life.

We swoon over each other, Gene and me,
survivors of a family implosion
that defied the era's norms, the *status quo*.
And we are survivors of a global explosion
that flung us, like Dorothy and Toto,
into the vortex of a counterculture tornado.

We visit our East and West Coasts,
our time together filled with praise, hope, and nostalgic laughter.
I remember him sneaking into the Augusta National Golf Course
stealing balls from water holes and selling them,
canoeing down the Savannah River in his mom-shocking Mohawk,
sprawling out his arms in Temptations dance routines with Phil,
worrying about buying Weejuns and Gant shirts for school
before he blew that off.

Wine is now his drug of choice,
and I can't believe my luck that I'm related to
this hetero man with a gay man's sensitivity,
an honorary girl we tell him, except when
his PTSD throws him into anger on the road.

This Renaissance pastiche human being
has the deep kindness of his sharecropper grandfather,
the tender empathy and generosity of his mother,
all rolled into his bluesy, spinning, I-feel-goodness,
that dances sunshine into cloudy days,
his fingers jitterbugging Allman Brothers instrumentals
on the strings of a stunning guitar
he has sculpted with his own soulful hands.

Georgia Sunset

Charcoal silhouettes of pines
jut against a lava red sky,
crimson presses pink
into white whispers of dandelions.
Quail sing to each other
as lightning bugs
turn the pasture into fairyland,
twinkling secrets
into the rising night.

Elaine walks to the weathered fence,
greets the gentle blond and gold palomino
prancing toward her in silent delight.
The mare nuzzles the cheek
of her *femina sapiens* old friend,
tosses her head with that equine grace
that captures the hearts of little girls.
Elaine stretches herself across
the last patch of sun-gold grass
as if modeling for Wyeth—
a Southern *Christina's World.*

Darkness tides in, floods red clay.
Green grass disappears under black waters.
As crickets alternate between
basso and soprano,
unseen honeysuckle scents the air.

Night's river drowns the forest,
soaks the clouds, and rising ever higher,
floods the sun, douses it.
We swim to safe haven
through these neap waters,

stoke a small fire in the fireplace.
We gather around it, warming ourselves
and drying out the darkness by flamelight.

Elaine is a hope-spinning artist
who draws stories for children
and wins awards for it,
who carves fawns and rabbits from foam,
watercoloring them to reality.

Elaine remembers excitement
standing next to a sign
over a water fountain when she is five.
She turns the fountain's handle,
expecting sweet, rainbow water
before a stern man tells her she is
drinking from the wrong one.

Tonight she is a woman coaxing the blues
from an acoustic guitar
fashioned by the man standing next to her
who will soon rip the sounds
of long-gone Duane Allman's "Little Martha"
from strings of his own guitar.

And at this day's end,
on their umpty-leventh anniversary,
the sun has painted
these twenty-first century
Renaissance hippies
a chiaroscuro masterpiece.

Greatmother

They are not dead who live in the hearts they leave behind.
—Tuscarora Native American Tribe Proverb

This has been the best week of my life
Mim says as she lies at home dying,
family and friends flocking by.
She says she is dying happy
she won't have to decide who
to vote for as President again.
Her children versus her Southern roots
left her flummoxed last time.

This afternoon the oxygen machine
hums, thumps, breathes
at the side of this woman who doesn't
notice it anymore as she sleeps off
the effects of her anti-cancer drugs
and her soothing of her stricken friends.

In the hospital she saw Kate for the last time—
Kate, now five, whose two-year-old mind
struggled to say *great grandmother*,
couldn't get it right— Kate who first looked
frightened by all the tubes and wires,
then sang her ABC song quietly as she drew
on the nurses' dry erase board,
asking what "rampage" meant
when the adults talked about the news.
At the end of an hour she was on the bed,
leaning in, listening to *Goodnight, Moon*,
offering Mim her stuffed rabbit,
snuggling past the I.V pole.

At five, Kate's greatmother was making biscuits,
and just after the Great Crash, she picked cotton
with her sharecropper mother, father, five brothers,
bent for hours, her seven-year-old fingers bleeding
as they struggled with prickly pods
beneath an unrelenting August sun.

You can tell me the truth she smiled,
trying to ease the difficult task of the doctors
who had poked at her pancreas,
made off with her blood.
I got tough in the cotton patch.
Every morning she has grits with an egg cooked in,
a pat of olive oil melted in the middle,
zesty black pepper snowed on top.
Before the nausea, grits is her best food friend,
red-eye gravy grits from the Wal-Mart across town.
This is the one thing she vows to take to Heaven—
if they aren't already there.

Mim pulls up her blanket and sheet,
shows off her pedicured toes— rich candy red.
She reminds herself of her independence day
when she arranged her own trip to the mall with *The Lift.*
She spent the day shopping and pampering herself,
no hint that ten days later she would
not be able to stand.

This morning she takes the yellow daisy
from her breakfast tray,
pencils it behind her ear,
wears her flower and a perky grin.
It is her first day of a steroid high— prednisone
to reverse an allergic reaction to the medicine
she's been taking to stop throwing up.
Can't she just stay on it? her son Gene pleads

after four days of drug-induced mania are over—
I don't have the energy to lift a chicken off the nest
she says, as she slams back to the planet where she's dying.

She cries for the fourth time on this jonesing morning.
Her first tears came three weeks before,
talking to her granddaughter who cannot come
from med school in Cuba. She cries when
her ophthalmologist calls to comfort her,
when her niece reads a memorializing poem.
On this come-down morning she sobs:
she has forgotten to eat the sausage biscuit
her son woke at six to make for her,
before leaving for work.

This silver-haired, 82-year-old version
of the mother whose great lake of empathy always
gave us a place to float, safe from forests of fear,
swamps of self-doubt, from the deserts of confusion
and hypocrisy in the culture around us,
this smooth-skinned, genteel Southern woman
applies lipstick, darkens her eyebrows a little,
takes out her blush, transforms from pale patient
to chic, rose-cheeked zen traveler.

She is ancient Inuit woman, *Greatmother,*
crinkling the corners of her eyes,
telling funny stories of her childhood,
comforting us as if we are her baby chicks
and she a nesting bird trying to warm us.

When she shifts onto her cold, new, breakaway home,
drifting into the Arctic Ocean, we watch her from shore.
As her silhouette dissolves below horizon's edge,
as the sky colors in afterglow,
the wings of a great Arctic snowy owl
unfold inside me.

High Point

Mozart melts our pre-wilderness stress—
the shotgun blast of the thermos crashing from the roof of the car
onto cold, hard asphalt, leaving a terminal dent;
the slow, gray, dawning reality: a trail guide left at home—
as we sway back and forth along the switchbacks
and ess curves of Highway 140
heading to Yosemite through El Portal.

Cheeky white clouds nibble the sizzling egg yolk sun
on our first day out; the next, we hike the high country
with snow salting our jackets. On the final day,
we rise, climb for hours— by car, on foot—
perch at dusk on a peak almost as high as
Half Dome, that stands across the valley from us.

Shivering in the chilled air
of this 360-degree Sierra-top view,
we watch the razor of horizon
slit the throat of sun:
the sky fills with blood.
This death stuns us, eclipses all,
takes us out someplace far away
from our pale lives.

We stumble down Sentinel Dome
along a sandy, rock-studded trail,
unsteady in fading light,
still mesmerized by the red nightfall,
and the cranberry and cornflower pastels
that echo on the other side of this universe.

The dinky stars of our flashlights
save us, and another pair of hikers,
from an all-night circling through evergreens.
Small, steady light of Jupiter
jewels the black sky as we reach our car,
sink into its seats for the long journey
down through the winding darkness.

A coyote streaks across the road
as the full moon rises.
We listen to Mozart again,
then, to the moonlit silence.

Birthday Blink

2014

> *A voice said, Look me in the stars*
> *And tell me truly, men of earth,*
> *If all the soul-and-body scars*
> *Were not too much to pay for birth.*
> —Robert Frost, "A Question"

From cotton fields,
through marshes of grief,
lifting into ethereal clouds
and a Tinkerbell aerie where
lifelong friendships hatch,
warming over two decades.

A scary fall
from the woven twigs and dreams
of that mountaintop nest,
a tumbling through trees,
toward bone crushing boulders,
bouncing into a lucky updraft
of fragrant winds,
a soft landing in a valley
of flowering Sapphic love,
home at last.

Our baby chicks fly, thrive
beyond silent wounds
from their parents' wildstyle.
They shine like first rays of morning sun,
while their old Potemkin village
twinkles, a starry night sky
of ambiguity,
just below their horizon.

I am four years on from
will you still need me,
two years before
terribly strange,
and if I could, I wouldn't
change a single crazy thing.

Fairy Rings

Occasionally, an almost perfect circle of redwood trees grows in the forest. These "fairy rings" or "family circles" sprout even if a redwood tree has been long logged or harvested, as its root system is still alive. ... Instead of growing deep, the giant tree's roots grow out, extending hundreds of feet laterally. Wrapping their roots around other redwood roots, these trees help each other stay in the ground.
—Brochure on Redwood Trees in a California State Park

As we head toward lunch at Alice's Restaurant near La Honda,
I think about the 1939 International Harvester school bus
starting its odyssey east from here to the 1964 New York World's Fair.
This Merry Pranksters' magic *Further*
set out fifty years ago this summer,
and after many memorable journeys,
many multi-colored art installations on its body,
it rusts now on a rural property somewhere in Oregon.

In old pictures you can see it covered in neon rainbows, goldfish,
a huge red rose, and succulent grapes dangling from green vines.
A tiger gazes near its right rear window,
and a spotted, white dog sits cool, wearing shades,
below hybrid Egyptian-psychedelic art and goofy hieroglyphics.

A hippie farmer with patched jeans holds a hoe in a garden
of starfish, stars, and the blue-green Earth.
Dorothy, Tin Man, Scarecrow, Lion, lock arms toward Oz,
Toto trailing, along a rippling ribbon of Yellow Brick Road.

A dark blue whale splashes in a white spray above a cerulean sea
next to Michelangelo's Sistine Adam floating on a deep magenta cloud.
The bus shouts *color!* in rich, pleasing hues
and its hubcaps are pastel— pink, white, light green, tangerine.

These neon Easter egg wheels roll on resurrection journeys across
       America
and beyond, zig-zagging throughout the day and night
with Neal Cassidy's meth-edged alertness steering.
They drive the whole country out of the fifties.

The two of us, in our last-decade's dusty, black, gas-lapping Civic,
are driving home from *The Love Shack* in Santa Cruz,
celebrating one of our sixty-something birthdays.
We have just come from a redwood forest where we lie on our backs
in the middle of a grove of trees called *Cathedral,*
looking up into blue sky at lacy, green needles
waltzing in the wind, backlit by sun—
a *fairy ring*, a perfectly round *redwood family circle.*

We talk about old friends, now spread from Hawaii to London and Wales,
about how our seedling communal lives have grown apart by thousands
      of miles.
We say the blessing we feel: no matter how far flung this once-close
      circle has grown,
our roots still touch, entwine, still hold us, help us *kiss the sky.*

45th Anniversary: Falling into Flowers (2014)

(Poem with lines from Abbie Hoffman)

...Today my son told me
that in the meadows,
at the edge of the heavy woods
in the distance, he saw
trees of white flowers.
I feel that I would like
to go there
and fall into those flowers
and sink into the marsh near them.
> — William Carlos Williams, from "The Widow's Lament in
> Springtime"

On the path to the eucalyptus forest
clothing the soft hills above my home,
forest where Ishi roamed
as the last of his mostly-massacred Yahi tribe,
eighty different kinds of flowers quiver in a lazy wind
against a backdrop of green shrubs and blue sky,
lifting their faces, like babies, to the round nourishment of the sun.

Brittlebush, Devil's Nettle, Little Apples, Little Feathers,
Mule Ears, Mountain Mahogany, Ithuriel's Spear, Indian Warrior.

Copas de oro, first gold of Russian explorers of the New World,
bright fields flecked with shimmering orange suns
blazing above bluffs where ship's hulls kiss the rocky coast—
windblown Golden Poppies.

Yerba Santa, Douglas Iris, Desert Bells, Golden Violets,
Western Azalea, Crape Myrtle, Matilija Poppy, Red Larkspur.

Morning Glory overgrowth, from the two-seat-swing porches
of my Southern roots, vines into this morning's walk,
on its way to envelop my future. You Heavenly Blue,
you Moonflower, you Brocade of Dawn, steeped in magic ergot.

Tidy Tips, Blue Lobelia, Johnny Jump Ups, Manzanita,
Pride of Madeira, Wood Rose, Red Flowering Currant, Marigold.

Acacia, whistling thorn tree, fills each spring
with yellow floral caterpillars I once traveled inside
on a long-ago, life-altering mushroom ride.
Dear forever-after soulmate, acacia,
at home along The Nile gracing Cleopatra's view
or along the staircase leading to a cobblestone street
above Parnassus, the Marin Headlands, the Golden Gate.

Crimson Columbine, Silver Wattle, Yellow Ginger, Lavender Cotton,
Wild Mock Orange, Daffodils, Leopard Lily, Goat's Beard.

Towers of inflorescence
fly up and down a simple stem—
Purple Chinese Houses, called Innocence—
petal-walled pagodas where a gentle, whispering wind
evokes old, hope-filled, laughing litanies
Pied-Pipering souls toward Bohemia:

Plans are being made to mine the East River with daffodils.
Dandelion chains are being wrapped around induction centers....
The cry of "Flower Power" echoes through the land.

Fairy Slippers, Common Yarrow, Purple Sage, Apricot Mallow,
Bird of Paradise, Meadow Foam, Flannel Bush, Primrose.

Apollo slips to earth to cherish handsome, young Hyacinth,
and as they toss a disc in emerald fields,
Zephyr gusts his jealous West Wind.

The discus rips beloved Hyacinth's head,
folding his body over Apollo's shoulder, dying.
Blood rivers into scarlet pools that soak the earth,
transform to royal blue and amethyst blooms,
each blossom bent earthward in a tender re-creation—
Hyacinth falling into Apollo's last embrace.

Lavender, Scarlet Sage, Wild Canterbury Bells, Lemon Geranium,
Japanese Maple, Gooseberry, Redwood Sorrel, Flowering Cherry.

Fairy Lanterns, Fiddleneck, Owl's Clover, Mission Bells,
Purple Larkspur, Purple Thistle, Jewelflowers, Blue Witch.

First love— blue shooting starflower
taken by a gust of black wind—
you, who left me with a longing for the marsh,
now thrive in transcendent, bluesy, trailside aura
as I walk the winding paths on this ancient hill
forty-five years from the year of your death.
The poison dusted all around us helped to kill you.
Your kind— our kind— suffered a decimation.

In Ishi's forest today, soft perfumes mingle in an ever brightening air,
and as I count purple, crimson, orange, gold, blue, lavender flower-flags,
fluttering in the warm wind rising inside this hopeful summer light,
I see you before your transformation into midnight warning,
you as morning sky's promise, you a shimmering forget-me-not
woven into the spring equinox. This is a canticle
to the enduring orchid bloom of troubled you;
you who spun me westward, electrifying my existence
with early grief's florid wisdom.

Grief

Between grief and nothing, I will take grief.
—William Faulkner

I.
Grief is discovering the world is flat after all,
that people really do fall off.

II.
Grief is a red-winged blackbird
that startles when it lands
in empty, outstretched hands—
delicate, feathery thing
that keeps coming back
in familiar patterns
like seasons, dreams.

Hold it tenderly when it lights,
despite its sharp claws,
and it will sing you
to another world,
then bring you home.

About the Author

Lynne Barnes was born in Georgia and moved to New York City in 1968 with a front row ticket to *Hair*, before migrating to San Francisco in 1969, two years after the Summer of Love. She has worked as a nurse on psych emergency units and oncology wards, and as a librarian in San Francisco's Public Libraries. She was part of a commune that thrived for twenty years in the Haight Ashbury. She lives with her beloved partner, Carole.

Gratitude

In early 1992, just after the commune I had lived in for twenty years disbanded, I read **Diane Wood Middlebrook**'s biography of **Anne Sexton** and I decided to begin writing poetry. I am grateful to these poet-teachers who have nourished me over the last twenty-five years:

Kim Addonizio, for saying "no, no, no" when it was needed, and inviting our little circle of poet wannabes into your home in San Francisco in 1992, when you were just starting to teach, years before your nomination for the National Book Award.

Ellen Bass, for charging my batteries again in Santa Cruz in the early 2000s, and for the inspiration of your lesbian sex poem splashed across America in the pages of *The New Yorker* in 2013.

Leslie Kirk Campbell, for being one of the first people to fold me into an encouraging writer's workshop... Ripe Fruit, a San Francisco institution.

Jack Hirschman, for publishing so many of my poems in the Friends of the San Francisco Public Library's *Poets 11* series over the years, and for the honor of the shine of your Beat legend light on me.

Dorianne Laux, for a memorable workshop in your home in the mid-90s.

Genny Lim, for your helpful feedback during that one hour I won with you in a contest years ago.

Clive Matson, for the magical poetry workshop at Wilbur Hot Springs in early '92, my first leap after reading Anne Sexton.

Len Sanazarro, poetry teacher and partner of treasured poet William Dickey, for your tender mentorship over the years at **City College of San Francisco.** You were beloved by your students and we are all still sad you are no longer with us.

Sarah Van Arsdale, for your encouragement as a poet and as editor of the University of California San Francisco (UCSF) *Synapse*; for that $10 check for my first published poem in 1994.

Dr. David Watts, for letting me be a part of your amazing *Poetry and Medicine* class at UCSF.

Mark Wunderlich, for your very special class at the Harvey Milk Institute.

Harvey Milk Institute writers' circle, Kim Addonizio's early circle of student poets, and to and my numerous **online poetry workshop mates over the years through Diane Frank's Blue Light Press.** Gratitude to these workshop buddies from the early days: **Michael Aleynikov, Ina Campbell, Liz Dossa, Barbara Epremian, Karen Hones,** and **Priscilla Lee.**

Special Thanks To:

Diane Frank, for your effervescent mentoring over the past eight years, and the examples of your own beautiful books and those of the other vibrant poets you publish at **Blue Light Press.**

Melanie Gendron, for laying out this book so beautifully with your artistic eye.

Carole Hay, my beloved, for your perfect "California Poppies" cover art.